THE VATICAN AGAINST ISRAEL:

J'ACCUSE

THE VATICAN AGAINST ISRAEL:

J'ACCUSE

BY GIULIO MEOTTI

mantua books

2013

Published by: Mantua Books Ltd.
Canada
www.mantuabooks.com
Email: administration@mantuabooks.com

Library and Archives Canada Cataloguing in Publication

Meotti, Giulio, author
        The Vatican against Israel : J'accuse / Giulio Meotti.

ISBN 978–1–927618–02–8 (pbk.)

        1. Catholic Church--Foreign relations--Israel. 2.
Israel--Foreign relations--Catholic Church. 3. Catholic
Church--Foreign relations--Arab countries. 4. Arab countries-
-Foreign relations--Catholic Church. 5. Christianity and
antisemitism. 6. Catholic Church and Zionism. 7. Arab-
Israeli conflict. 8. Jews--Persecutions--History.

I. Title.

BX1628.M46 2013   327.456'3405694   C2013-906899-6

Cover Illustration & Design by David B. Strutt

This book is dedicated to my wife and children, without whose love I could not have written this book.

Praise for
The Vatican Against Israel:
J'ACCUSE

"This new book by Giulio Meotti shows once again that if there were a contemporary list of 'Righteous Gentiles' whose heroism consists of fighting with all their intellectual and moral might both against the remnants of the old anti-Semitism and the newer mutation that disguises itself as anti-Zionism, his name would surely be very near the top."

- Norman Podhoretz, writer

"I have great respect for Giulio Meotti."

- Guy Milliere, University of Paris

"Heroic archival research and aggressive interviewing has been conducted by Giulio Meotti. He has given no peace to those enemies of the peace of Israel, the bishops and other leaders of the local Roman Catholic communities in Israel, who are responsible for winning the Vatican over to Palestinian anti-history and to Anti-Zionism – the current form of the anti-Judaism that governed Roman Catholic attitudes towards Israel for two millennia and still governs it today."

- Paul Merkley, Professor Emeritus of History, Carleton University, Ottawa

"Meotti's work is astonishing: Brave, enlightening, and frankly, gut-wrenching... Meotti is a heroic truth-teller."

-Phyllis Chesler, best-selling author

"While many cheered a "new phase" in the Catholic Church's view of the establishment of and support for the State of Israel following Nostra Aetate, Giulio Meotti's journalistic tenacity elucidates in pellucid terms that historical facts cannot be fudged. Meotti baldly describes in clear terms that there is little difference, if any, between classical anti-Semitism and its modern manifestation, anti-Zionism. A must read for those who wish to plumb the depths of the Church's antipathy toward the national right of Jewish statehood."

-Rabbi Jonathan Hausman

"Giulio Meotti combines astute investigative reporting and passionate intellectual courage in his compelling analysis of The Vatican's hypocritical campaign to delegitimize Israel. The bitter, tragic irony is that these perfidious efforts--borne of a toxic brew of delusive Islamophilia, and residual Judeophobia-- will likely be more destructive to The Church and its votaries, than the uniquely resilient Jewish State."

Dr. Andrew G. Bostom, author and Associate Professor of Medicine at Brown University Medical School

TABLE OF CONTENTS

ACKNOWLEDGEMENTS

I cannot name all who should be named. I am indebted to Howard Rotberg of Mantua Books, because he always believed in the importance of this book. No author could have asked for a better publisher. Howard is also a very rare moral voice. I must thank Giuliano Ferrara, who created the most beautiful newspaper in the world. A special word must be written for Professor Hillel Weiss, he helped me find the right way forward. I thank my parents, who taught me to respect myself and my word.

—*Giulio Meotti*

1. INTRODUCTION: A SCANDAL NAMED "ISRAEL"

For over 100 years, and half a century after the Holocaust, the Catholic Church has been hostile to the creation of a Jewish homeland. Chaim Weizmann, who would become the first president of the State of Israel, complained in 1922, that "the Vatican is moving Heaven and Earth against us."

For the Vatican, an independent Jewish State bearing the name "Israel," with Jerusalem as its capital, and a renewal of life in the land of the Bible, has been the most complex theological Christian problem and scandal to Church dogma. A vital Jewish people restored after 2,000 years to its own holy land has raised unsolved questions about the meaning of Church history and teachings.

For sixty years after the Jewish State gained independence in 1948, the Vatican adopted a policy fitting to Israel's Arab-Islamic enemies: total non-recognition of Jewish statehood and peoplehood. Despite acceptance by every Western nation and even, at one time, by the Communist bloc, Israel was not accorded diplomatic recognition by the Vatican before 1993. But even now that the Vatican and the State of Israel have formal diplomatic ties, the Catholic Church is rarely able even to mention the Jewish State. It is no secret that today Catholic tourist maps and pilgrimage brochures omit the name "Israel," using instead the sanitized expression "Holy-Land" or even "Palestine." This is one visible effect of Catholic "replacement theology," which adopted a de-Judaizing language.

When Pope John Paul II traveled to Israel in 2000, the Vatican requested the Jewish authorities to remove the Star of David from the ambulances that escorted the Pope.[1] When the pontiff ascended to the Temple Mount in Jerusalem, Judaism's most holy site, he wasn't welcomed by any Israeli official, but by representatives of the Palestinian Authority, and the holy complex was bedecked in Arab flags. It was an implicit recognition of Muslim hegemony. It was taken to mean that Islam and Christianity superseded the Jewish religion and have the right to "inherit" its holy places. "The Holy See's taking a stance as the ally of the heads of the Palestinian Authority in the place most holy to the Jewish people, is therefore almost a fait accompli."[2]

In 1955 the Israel Philharmonic Orchestra played before Pope Pius XII. The Vatican agreed to the appearance of the orchestra "as a tribute to the Catholic Church for saving Jews during the Holocaust." Eliyahu Sasson, then the Israeli representative in Rome, was willing to allow the orchestra to perform before the Pope on the Shavuot Jewish holiday. Finally the orchestra performed Beethoven's Seventh Symphony before the Pope. But on the next day the official Vatican newspaper, L'Osservatore Romano, reported that "his Holiness met with Jewish musicians from 14 different nations," without any mention of the State of Israel.[3]

The Vatican knew that the Israeli Orchestra was a special symbol of the Jewish renaissance. In 1936 Bronislaw Huberman put his violin in his case and left Warsaw to begin a long journey. Huberman said to his fellow musicians: "Come with me to Tel Aviv, something terrible is going to happen in Europe." The violinists and pianists who did not believe Huberman were murdered in the gas chambers. That was the beginning of the Israeli orchestra directed by Arturo Toscanini on its debut. During the 1948 war, Leonard Bernstein led the orchestra in Beersheba. All around there were boys and girls with guns on their shoulders

---

[1] "The Holy Land, in an edgy mood, awaits the Pope's visit," New York Times, March 19, 2000

[2] "Arafat Is the Host - On the Temple Mount," by Nadav Shragai, Ha'aretz, March 5 2000

[3] "Israel-Vatican Relations 1948-1973: The Israeli Perspective," by Amnon Ramon (Santa Croce conference on Israel-Vatican relations, June 2012)

and the music of Ravel and Mozart in their ears. During the 1967 war, an Indian conductor, Zubin Mehta, arrived in Israel on a plane loaded with ammunition. It was the only way to reach the Jewish State. In 1991, when Saddam Hussein's rockets hit Tel Aviv, the auditorium was full of people. Mehta, a non-Jew, was playing Bach when the siren started to sound. He wore a gas mask. Another musical virtuoso, Isaac Stern, was performing when a rocket was fired from Baghdad. Stern stood his ground and calmed the people in the auditorium with a solo Bach Sarabande. In the face of such bravery by the musicians, the Pope made no statements of support.

On January 5, 1964, Pope Paul VI made for the first time in history, a papal visit in the Middle East. The Pope said in Megiddo where he entered Israel, "We are coming as pilgrims, we come to venerate the Holy Places; we come to pray."[4] The Pope thanked unspecified "authorities" and refused to address Zalman Shazar as "Mr. President,"avoiding any mention of that damned word "Israel." On his return to the Vatican, Paul sent a thank you note to "Mr. Shazar" in Tel Aviv — not Jerusalem, the capital of the State of Israel. To exorcise the Israeli devil, they refuse to name it *expressis verbis*. Pope Paul VI spent only 11 hours in Israel. He avoided Israeli-controlled West Jerusalem, refusing to meet with the chief rabbi, Yitzhak Nissim.[5] A few years later, Nissim attacked Pope Paul VI for his implied criticism of Israel's reprisal raid on Beirut Airport and accused the Pope and the Vatican of conducting a "general campaign" against the Jewish religion and the Jewish people. The Chief Rabbi alleged that the Pope was not moved by the lives lost in the terrorist bombing of the Machane Yehuda market place in Jerusalem a month earlier "but he hurried to console Lebanon after the destruction of a few planes without loss of life."[6]

---

[4] "The Land, the Bible, and History," by Alain Marchadour and David Neuhaus, Fordham University Press, 2010
[5] "Israel Recalls '64 Papal Visit," Chicago Tribune, March 19 2000
[6] http://www.jta.org/1969/01/03/archive/rabbi-nissim-assails-pope-paul-for-criticism-of-israeli-reprisals

As historian Daniel Goldhagen stated,[7] after the Holocaust the Catholic Church, which has a profound influence on more than one billion Christians around the world, had the moral duty to defend Israel and to make the world a safer place for the remaining Jewish communities. This book shows that the Vatican tragically failed, and has forsaken the Jews again. The Jewish State has been abandoned by the Vatican in its most tragic times after the Holocaust, the Six-Day War, the Yom Kippur War, the Gulf War, two barbaric Intifadas, the Lebanese War in 2006, and the war against Hamas in 2009. In 2004 the bishops of England and Wales released a note to Christian pilgrims in the holy land not to take an Israeli bus "the day after a sheikh is assassinated."[8] The Jews were left alone on the buses, and Israeli mothers had to decide to send their children using means of transport other than what they themselves used, to save at least one part of the family in the event of an attack.

Why doesn't the Vatican raise its voice against Iran's incitement toward Israel's destruction, in which Israel has been called "cancer," "microbe," "filthy" and "rat"? Why is the Catholic Church fighting to make Judea and Samaria, Israel's strategic and historic mountains, "Judenrein" — free of Jews?[9] These are the Biblical areas that contained the great cities of the two previous Jewish commonwealths, such as Shiloh (where the Tabernacle stood for hundreds of years), Beit El (where Jacob had his vision of the ladder) and Hebron (where Abraham, Isaac and Jacob are buried with their wives Sarah, Rebecca and Leah).

In 1974 the Vatican implicitly recognized the Palestinian Liberation Organization, but not the State of Israel. It took twenty years to do that. We should not see as natural the fact that different Popes refused to recognize Israel for fifty years after its foundation. The Jewish State was not even mentioned in the

[7] "A moral reckoning" by Daniel Goldhagen, Vintage 2003
[8] "You may choose not to go on an Israeli bus after a sheikh has been assassinated," Catholic Herald, May 7, 2004
[9] "Vatican body to ask UN to end 'Israeli occupation'," Ynet News, October 23, 2010

famous "Nostra Aetate" declaration of 1965, in the "Guidelines" of 1974 or in any Papal statement before the 1980s. The Vatican had normal ties, however, with the most oppressive and odious regimes on this earth. It even maintained diplomatic relations with Nazi Germany until the very end of the war. Apparently, the Vatican considered only the State of Israel undeserving of its recognition.

"We note in shock the Pope's eagerness to recognize the Palestinian State before it has even yet arisen and we recall the eagerness of another Pope to recognize the Nazi regime four months after it was established,"[10] wrote the Israeli intellectual, lawyer and Knesset member Eliakim Haetzni in a petition published a few days before the Pope's visit to Israel in 2000. "We sense a profound sorrow over the fact that Pope John Paul, in demanding the internationalization of Jerusalem, is essentially following in the footsteps of Pope Pius XII, the person whose resounding silence when confronting the Holocaust, will never be forgotten nor forgiven, and who immediately upon the establishment of Israel, demanded the internationalization of Jerusalem."

With a long history of *Contra Judaeos* literature, there is now a new genre of *Contra Israel* discourse that has spread among the Vatican officials and Popes.[11] The tensions that characterize the relationship between the Vatican and Israel have their roots in the historical relationship between Catholicism and Judaism.

On January 25, 1904, Theodor Herzl, the founder of Zionism, obtained an audience in Rome with Pope Pius X to seek the Catholic support for the Jewish return to Zion. Herzl outlined his plans. The Pope's answer was clear: "We cannot give approval to this movement... We can never sanction it... The Jews have not recognized our Lord; therefore we cannot recognize the Jewish

---

[10] http://blog.womeningreen.org/?cat=48
[11] "Our Hands are Stained with Blood" by Michael L. Brown, Destiny Image, 1992

people. If you come to Palestine and settle your people there, we want to have Churches and priests ready to baptize all of you."[12]

As the Pope made clear to Herzl,[13] the existence of a restored Israel in the land of the Bible, proof that the Jewish people is not annihilated, assimilated and withering away is the living refutation of the Christian myth about the Jewish end in the historic process. And this is precisely why the State of Israel has been the most dramatic challenge for the Vatican and the biggest crisis for contemporary Christian theology. For centuries before the Shoah it was asserted (with different amounts of force at different times) that all Jews, both at the time of Christ and subsequently, bore the guilt of "deicide," or God-murder, and were therefore under a perpetual curse. By founding the State of Israel, the Jews were acting as though their punishment had been temporary. By regaining its sovereignty, the Jewish people, who until now had been a witness to the truth of Christianity, instead became witness to its *un*truth.

Never before had Christianity confronted such a theological conundrum. That is why in the most influential quarters of Christianity, not only Catholicism, the Jews are still regarded as an apostate group, not entitled to defend itself from genocidal terrorism. The second Vatican Council partially revoked this horrible, proto-Holocaust blood libel only in 1965. Then "the Vatican glided all too easily from anti-Semitism to anti-Zionism. The same Church that would not recognize Israel opened quasi-diplomatic relations with the PLO. John Paul II even permitted himself to be photographed embracing Yasser Arafat."[14]

The same Church that didn't recognize Israel opened diplomatic relations with the PLO, a terror organization whose goal is the "liberation" of the Holy Land from the Jews who live between the

---

[12] Lowenthal, Marvin (Ed). "The Diaries of Theodor Herzl," Grosset and Dunlap, New York, 1962

[13] "Herzl e Sokolov in Vaticano" in "Scritti sull'ebraismo in memoria di G. Bedarida" by Nahon N., Firenze, 1966

[14] "Has the Catholic Church really embraced Israel?," National Post, January 15, 1994

Mediterranean and the Jordan River — the same Arafat who had killed more civilians than Osama bin Laden. The Church formally recognized Israel's existence only two decades after Israel's foe, Egypt, signed a peace treaty with the Jewish State. The Vatican was the first state to recognize the Federal Republic of Germany, the heir of Third Reich, but one of the last to recognize Israel.[15] The Vatican had diplomatic relations with over 130 states. It acknowledged their legitimacy even as it disputed, in some cases, their borders.

Why has such a different standard been applied to Israel?

On the morning of 30 December 1993, in the Vatican's Sala Regia, the Fundamental Agreement was signed by Claudio Celli, Vatican Assistant Secretary of State, and Yossi Beilin, Israel's Deputy Minister of Foreign Affairs, paving the way toward diplomatic relations between the two parties.[16] But as Archbishop Pietro Sambi, who served as the Vatican nuncio to Israel, declared in 2007, "To be frank, relations between the Catholic Church and the state of Israel were better when there were no diplomatic relations."[17] The diplomatic relations between Israel and the Vatican created the illusion of normalcy. Despite the formal agreement, the Vatican is still 'at war' with the State of Israel when it deals with military self-defense, global anti-Semitism, Jewish attachment to the land, Islamic rejectionism, support for Arab irredentism, a retrograde Catholic anti-Zionist theology, and a strategic terrorist campaign against Israeli civilians.

A significant part of this book deals with Arab Christian anti-Semitism and the hatred promoted against Israel by the Eastern bishops. Many scholars dismiss their anti-Judaism and anti-Zionism as a product of their Arab identity. This is a racist explanation, which only means that an Arab can't live in peace with the Jews. It is also like saying that the Vatican's responsibility

---

[15] "Cross on the Star of David" by Uri Bialer, Indiana University Press, 2005
[16] "The Vatican-Israel Accords: Political, Legal and Theological Contexts," edited by Marshall Breger, Notre Dame, 2004
[17] Reuters, November 21, 2007

during the Holocaust had nothing to do with what the Churches did in Bratislava, Prague, Belgrade, Warsaw, or Paris.

Because of their proximity to Christianity's holy sites, these Arab bishops have ready access to visiting Christian leaders in the West who are all too willing to accept a distorted narrative about the Arab-Israeli conflict. Palestinian Christians have long been among Israel's most vocal critics, using every opportunity to portray the Jewish state as a malevolent force. And most of the time the Catholic Church 'speaks' through its local clergy.

The Vatican's criminalization of Zionism, which the Arab Churches made a basic condition of the Muslim-Christian rapprochement, still confers on the elimination of the Jewish State a priority over defending the rights of their own beleaguered Christian communities, which have been massacred and squeezed under Islamic rulers or Arab autocracies. Since the second half of the 20th century, it is the local Arab clergy who represent Western Christendom within the Arab Palestinian churches. As mentioned above, the Vatican speaks through them in the Middle East, and from the Middle East to the entire world.

Since 1967, when Israel captured its historical and biblical lands known as Judea and Samaria, the Catholic Churches have adopted a policy which aimed at forming a united front against Israel by identifying with the Arab cause. They strove to associate the Christian world in solidarity with the Palestinians and to promote a powerful anti-Zionist campaign in the West. The "Justice and Peace Commission," a Catholic body established in 1971, emphasizes in its pamphlets and sermons the common cause of Muslims and Christians against Israel and the Jews.[18]

As historian Bat Ye'or explained, the "Jewish peril" of pre-Shoah Christianity was reincarnated for post-Shoah Christianity in the State of Israel, with its corollary of the sacralization of the Arab Palestinians' cause and the demonization of "the Zionists." The most radical submission to Islamist demands has been the "de-

---

[18] "Islam and Dhimmitude" by Bat Ye'or, 2002, pp. 241

Zionization" of the Bible, which took place in the Arab Churches by eliminating the word "Zion" and "Israel" from religious texts. It is the same process undertaken by the German Churches in the 1930s. In 1988 the Anglican synod of New Zealand even removed the words "Zion" and "Israel" from the Psalter.[19] In a 2013 report titled "The Inheritance of Abraham? The Promised Land," the Church of Scotland says Israel does not belong to the Jewish people. "Promises about the land of Israel were never intended to be taken literally, or as applying to a defined geographical territory," it says. "The 'Promised Land' in the Bible is not a place, so much as a metaphor of how things ought to be among the people of God. This 'Promised Land' can be found, or built, anywhere." The New Testament, the report states, contains a "radical re-interpretation" of the concepts of "Israel," "temple," "Jerusalem," and "land."

For Abbé Moubarac, one of the most important representatives of the Eastern Catholicism, Israel's liberation of Jerusalem in 1967 was a "rape" and a "ritual crime." For Moubarac, Israel represents a sacrilege since it had broken the vocation assigned it by Islam; and it would be through the mediation of the Islamic vocation for Jerusalem that – through a Muslim-Christian union – the destruction of Zionism and the return of the Jews to exile would be fulfilled. Anti-Zionism today is made up of three strands: Muslim, Secular and Christian. After Vatican II, Arab Catholics returned to the deicide theme. It was after "Nostra Aetate" that the Christological themes of Palestinianism developed based on the Judeophobic schemas of the crucifixion. The Arab Churches, supported by the Vatican, transfigured Palestinian terrorism into a Christ-like image.

A new assassination of the Jews was again allowed during the Second Intifada. 2,000 Israeli civilians paid with their lives. On December 11, 2000 – two weeks before the Christmas Jubilee and during the first weeks of Palestinian war against Israeli civilians and

---

[19] "New Zealand Church Rejects Liturgy Change Urged by Jews," Jewish Telegraphic Agency, August 21, 1992

military forces – the Palestinian daily "Intifada" displayed a caricature showing a crucified woman called "Palestine."[20] No Church body reacted before or after Christmas to this blood libel against the Jews and Israel at the close of the Jubilee Year of 2000. As this book shows, not only did the Vatican never refute the Palestinian propaganda about Christianity, but many of its officials and bishops support it. As Moubarac had defined it, the Christian theological compassion for the Jews had to be accompanied by an unremitting war against Israel and Zionism. This identification of Israel with evil assigned the symbol of good to Palestine. Israel liberated the European conscience from the culpability of anti-Semitism and the Shoah, allowing a justification for a new battle against the Jews.

According to the narrative offered by the Vatican authorities, "peace" is contingent on Israeli concessions and efforts to dismantle the Jewish State. Vatican leaders use deicide imagery in reference to Israel, they portray Israel's efforts to prevent civilian casualties as "collective punishment,"[21] without mentioning Hamas, Fatah and Islamic Jihad's war crimes. Israel is associated with "militarism," "colonialism," and "injustice." The Vatican is becoming an unabashed apologist for Arab rejectionism, wrapping genocidal violence against Israelis in the mantle of innocents suffering and caricaturing the Jews as a divinely forsaken people, superseded in God's favor by "New Israel," stripped of any right to a land or a future.

In 1983 the Vatican Justice and Peace Commission published a pamphlet entitled "Muslims and Christians on the road together," emphasizing unity against Israel. The Vatican also sponsored centers, as well as publications, which stressed Arab Christian and Muslim unity. Today anti-Zionism is spread in the same way as was the traditional anti-Semitism diffused by the Churches in the XIX and XX centuries — by sermons, circulars, directives, and silences.

---

20 "Yasser's terrorist Jesus," Frontpage, November 15, 2004
21 "Vatican envoy urges Israel to refrain from collective punishment in Gaza," The Jerusalem Post, January 17, 2008

Palestinianism, as set out by numerous Catholic clergymen, draws on the two theological elements of anti-Judaism: "supersessionism" — the idea that Muslim-Christian unity replaced Israel — and the demonization of Jews for seizing a country which was not theirs. It is the blood libel of Israel's "occupation" with the return to the Catholic cycle of existential denial in which Israel is not *Israel*, but the usurper of an identity, of a history, of a name and of a land. A Middle Eastern version of liberation theology, supported by high profile Catholic clergy, presents the Palestinian Christians as "the true Israel," oppressed by a malevolent occupation government of theologically cursed Jews. Arab Christians who promote this obscurantist theology seek to curry favor with Muslims by accusing Israelis of "ethnic cleansing" and "Judaizing" Jerusalem. They always receive a sympathetic hearing in Europe and among the Western Churches.

Take Cardinal Gianfranco Ravasi, President of the Vatican Council for Culture, when commenting on the war between Israel and Hamas in 2012, delivered a severe attack on the Jewish people: "I think of the 'massacre of the innocents'. Children are dying in Gaza, their mothers' shouts is a perennial cry, a universal cry."[22] This high official of the Catholic Church implicitly equated Israel's operation in Gaza against terror groups with the New Testament story of Herod's slaughter of Jewish babies in his effort to kill Jesus. In 2005, while the synagogue of Netzarim in the Gaza Strip was burned by Arab terrorists, the Catholic Church stood silent despite Israeli rabbis' pleas to condemn the torching.

The Vatican rapprochement with the Jewish people after the Holocaust, and especially after the Nostra Aetate, took place at two levels, which the Vatican separated: theological and political. Each advance on the first level was counterbalanced by a deeper regression on the second, as if the two movements were synchronized. The closer the Vatican seemed to draw toward reconciliation and dialogue with Judaism, the louder grew the

---

[22] "Papa: card.Ravasi, grido 'strage innocenti' risuona in vittime Gaza," Asca News Agency, November 20 2012

clamor supporting the Arab cause against Israel. During the last fifty years, the Vatican authorities obfuscated the reality of a Jewish State, awaiting the disappearance of this vulnerable state seen by them as a malevolent accident of history.

This book not only urgently matters to all Jews, but also to Christians, since the two religions share a common scripture and moral values. Jesus was Jewish, and, for better or for worse, Jews and Christians have lived together in Europe and Middle East for 2000 years. In many parts of the Christian world there has been a rediscovery by Christians both of their Jewish roots and of the Jewishness of Jesus that is instructive as a historical phenomenon and has historic implications, both positive and negative, for Jewish-Christian relations. Christians have learned that Jesus was an observant Jew; he was circumcised, he attended the synagogue and he participated in the worship of the God of Israel administered by the priesthood on the Temple Mount in Jerusalem. His concerns with concepts like "the kingdom of God" or repentance, was the concern of the Jewish groups of his day. It is only after the death of Jesus, when his followers began to spread their new beliefs in the Greco-Roman world, that Christianity emerged as something separate, different and against Judaism.[23] So this is a story of symbiosis and rejection, affection and alienation. How the Vatican will relate to the State of Israel will also affect the future of the relationship between Christians and Jews.

After the Shoah, the theological challenge was to develop an authentic expression of Christianity that preserved the fundamentals of Christian faith and belief while eliminating supersessionism and the teaching of contempt. This kind of theological innovation has come to be known as "Post-Holocaust Christian theology."

Today all the largest Catholic forums, most of the high ranking bishops, and all of Arab Christianity, are immersed in a radical anti-Israel rhetoric that resembles that of the 30's and the Middle

[23] "The Crucified Jew: Twenty Centuries of Christian Anti-Semitism" by Cohn-Sherbok, Dan, William B. Eerdmans Publishing Company, 1997

Ages. Persistent cases of anti-Semitism amongst high ranking Catholics continue. Cardinal Oscar Andres Rodriguez Maradiaga, one of a small number of likely candidates to succeed Pope Benedict, has blamed the "Jewish media"[24] for the scandal surrounding the sexual misconduct of priests toward young parishioners. In an interview with the Italian-Catholic publication 30 Giorni, the cardinal claimed Jews influenced the media to exploit the controversy regarding sexual abuse by Catholic priests in order to divert attention from the Israeli-Palestinian crisis. Rodriguez then goes on to compare the Jewish-controlled media with "Hitler," because they are "protagonists of what I do not hesitate to define as a persecution against the Church."

Listen to Maradiaga's words:

"It certainly makes me think that in a moment in which all the attention of the mass media was focused on the Middle East, all the many injustices done against the Palestinian people, the print media and the TV in the United States became obsessed with sexual scandals that happened 40 years ago, 30 years ago. Why? I think it is also for these motives: What is the church that has received Arafat the most times and has most often confirmed the necessity of the creation of a Palestinian state? What is the church that does not accept that Jerusalem should be the indivisible capital of the State of Israel, but that it should be the capital of the three great monotheistic religions?"

Or take George Saliba, the Syriac Orthodox Church's bishop in Lebanon, who in an interview with Al-Dunya TV on July 24, 2011, declared that "the source... behind all these movements, all these civil wars, and all these evils" in the Arab world is nothing other than Zionism, "deeply rooted in Judaism."[25] The Jews, he says, are responsible for financing and inciting the turmoil in accordance with The Protocols of the Elders of Zion. These remarks are not an isolated case among Middle Eastern Christians. Thousands of Jews have died in Europe because of The Protocols of Elders of

---

[24] The Jewish Chronicle, 7 April 2010
[25] The Jerusalem Post, August 1, 2011

Zion, a short book concocted by czarist secret police in the 1890s and presented as minutes of a secret meeting during which Jews plotted world domination. Hitler used it as a manual in his war to exterminate the Jews. The constant use of the "Protocols" in the Arab media, especially in Telenovellas during the viewing month of Ramadan, creates an ambience in which any charge against the Jews is readily believed. Now the Christian clergy is fuelling anti-Jew hatred again using the "Protocols."

In January 2011, echoing the "Protocols," the Metropolitan Seraphim of Piraeus in a morning show on Greece's most popular TV channel declared that "there is a conspiracy to enslave Greece and Christian Orthodoxy." He also accused "International Zionism" of trying to destroy the family unit. When the bishop was then asked, "Why do you disagree with Hitler's policies? If they are doing all this, wasn't he right in burning them?," the bishop replied, "Adolf Hitler was an instrument of world Zionism and was financed from the renowned Rothschild family with the sole purpose of convincing the Jews to leave the shores of Europe and go to Israel to establish the new Empire."[26] One of the conspiracy theories against the Jews is that Rothschild wrote the "Protocols." The Metropolitan then wrote a letter of "clarification": "My vehement public opposition to International Zionism refers to the organization that is the successor of the 'Sanhedrin,' which through the Talmud, the Rabbinical Writings and Kabbalah has altered the faith of the Patriarchs, the Prophets and Righteous of the Jewish nation into Satanism," he went on to say. So according to the leader of the Christian Greek community, the Jews have been lead into Satanism by the teachings of the Talmud, the Rabbis and the Kabbalah, and Zionism is a conspiracy to take over the world.

Father Manuel Musalam, the head of the Catholic church in Gaza appointed by the Vatican authorities, has also used the "Protocols" to incite hatred against the Jews: "The Jew has a

[26] "Anti Defamation League Urges Greek Orthodox Church to Condemn Bishop's Blatant Anti-Semitism," December 22, 2010

principle from which we suffer and which he tries to impose on people: the principle of the 'gentiles.' To him, the gentile is a slave. They (the Jews) give the Palestinians working in Israel only a piece of bread, and tell them: 'This piece of bread that you eat is taken from our children, and we give it to you so you will live not as free men on your land, but as a proletariat and slaves in Israel, to serve us...'. The Protocols of the Elders of Zion are based on this principle, and anyone who reads the Protocols feels that we are in this period with the Jews ..."[27]

The greatest blood libel feeding anti-Jewish hate is enduring with the complicity of Christian bishops. Today there are very few leaders in the Vatican who consciously and publicly embrace anti-Semitism; yet words and actions of most of the Vatican officials, including the Popes, are usually hostile to Israel and Jews. They know that sophisticated anti-Semitism masks itself in apparently benign garb. Within the Church, there are growing numbers of leaders who dislike Israel because they believe that Jews are not entitled to any part of the Holy Land. Indeed, they feel that a Jewish state is both theologically "illegitimate" and intrinsically "racist."

The pro-Palestinian mantra, epitomized by humanitarian Catholic organizations such as Caritas and Pax Christi, assumes that Arabs are the innocent "victims" of Israeli occupation. The corollary is that they are a priori exculpated from any responsibility for their plight, especially terrorism against civilians, including the use of suicide bombers and rockets. The fact that the Arab states, the United Nations, and the Palestinian leadership itself have deliberately allowed the exiles of 1948 to rot in refugee camps is conveniently ignored; only the Jews are to blame.

Take the major Catholic NGO Trócaire,[28] the official overseas development agency of the Vatican in Ireland. Funders include the Government of Ireland. Trócaire, in its programs related to the

---

[27] "Arab Christian Clergymen Against Western Christians, Jews, and Israel," Memri, May 1, 2002

[28] "Misdirected Catholic Aid from Ireland fuels conflict," Ngo Monitor, March 18 2009

Arab-Israeli conflict, displays a consistent bias, including the "campaign on the illegal Wall" and "Exile Remembered: Israel, Palestine, and the Nakba – 60 years on," marking the "750,000 people...made homeless during the foundation of the Israeli state." Trócaire's website refers to the "Nakba or catastrophe – the start of a process of dispossession which continues today." During the Gaza operation, Trócaire called for "the suspension of the EU-Israel Association Agreement."

Trócaire has been awarded many prestigious prizes, such as the Hugh O'Flaherty International Humanitarian Award, in honor of "The Pimpernel of the Vatican," and colleagues who saved over 6,500 prisoners of war, Jews and citizens of Rome during the Nazi occupation.

But this famous Catholic NGO is also one of the most virulent demonizers of the Jewish State. After a campaign by Richard Humphreys, Labor party Councilor for Stillorgan, near Dublin, the Catholic NGO removed the material for schools titled "Give peace a chance," because it is full of anti-Israel stereotypes. In an op-ed in the Irish Times, Trócaire's director, Justin Kilcullen, urged his country to promote a total ban on "illegal settlement goods" and to "push European counterparts for similar action."

As exposed by the Israeli NGO Monitor group, Trócaire's "Occupied Palestinian Territories/Israel Programme Officer" Garry Walsh was previously employed as the National Coordinator for Ireland Palestinian Solidarity Campaign. Trócaire asks for a review of the EU-Israel association agreement. The initiative comes from the Bishop of Clonfert and chairman of Trócaire, Dr. John Kirby, and Bishop Ray Field, chairman of the Irish Commission for Justice and Social Affairs, both members of an international Catholic Church delegation to the Holy Land. The Catholic NGO castigated Israel for being an apartheid state which practices "racial segregation."

Along with a ban within Ireland, Trócaire is seeking a push towards an EU-wide ban of Israel's goods.

A document which was circulated by the Irish bishops on the Middle East accuses Israel of "the expulsion of over 750,000 Palestinians from their homes," the "forceful expropriation of land," the "plan to ensure that Jerusalem becomes ethnically a Jewish city," and the "refusal to recognize the applicability of the Fourth Geneva Convention."

The Catholic NGO is affiliated with many Palestinian groups such as the Palestinian Centre for Human Rights, which accuses Israel of "torturing" prisoners.

Trócaire is just one of the many NGOs which are now campaigning against Israel and the Jews. Another one is Pax Christi. Pax Christi has mounted a campaign to boycott Israeli products, including setting up stands in German pedestrian zones to encourage people to not buy Israeli goods.[29] Recently, Pax Christi sponsored the campaign "Occupation Tastes Bitter" demanding "unambiguous labeling of products from Israeli settlements."

During the Second Intifada Palestinian terrorists entered the Church of Nativity in Bethlehem. A group of activists of the International Solidarity Movement evaded Israeli military patrols and entered the Church to support the Arab terrorists. "Pax Christi USA," while not participating directly in ISM action, offered them a large public relations platform and sent a special "observer" in the person of Dennis B. Warner, Pax Christi USA.

The position of the NGO has been eloquently summarized by its chairman, the Italian Bishop Luigi Bettazzi: "To the Israeli friends I say: be aware that one day it will be said that the Nazis have been exceeded, that they killed ten for one of them and you killed a hundred."[30]

Another powerful Catholic NGO comes from the Netherlands, Cordaid, has been involved in financing the largest anti-Jewish hate campaign of the century, the UN World Conference against

---

[29] "German Jewish leader slams boycott activity," Jerusalem Post, August 2, 2012
[30] Migliaia ad Assisi "In Medio Oriente due popoli, due stati," L'Unità, January 18, 2009

Racism in Durban, South Africa. According to René Grotenhuis, director of the aid group Cordaid, "boycott of Israel in Palestine is justified."[31]

Another aid group is the Pontifical Mission for Palestine. One of its leaders in the region, Sami El-Yousef, just promoted a document saying that, "the Israeli occupation of Palestinian land is a sin against God and humanity," while the NGO former president, Robert Stern, gave an interview to an Italian monthly magazine under the headline: "Concentration Camps for Palestinians."

Then there is the Caritas NGO, the Vatican humanitarian arm, which gives relief to many people around the world, but when it comes to Israel, is very anti-Semitic. A poster graphically attacking the Israeli security fence featured Vatican headquarters address and listed the endorsement of 151 of Caritas' international branches. According to the Simon Weisenthal Center, "the poster undoubtedly exacerbates Middle East-related anti-Semitism, justifies further attacks on Jewish targets under the sanctification cover of the Holy See and impugns Caritas' credibility as an effective relief and unbiased relief agency."[32] In the Italian website of Caritas there is a link to "Stop the Wall," the so called "Palestinian Popular Campaign against the Wall of Apartheid."

In XIX century France, Catholic anti-Semites bore names such as "Ligue Antisemitique," "Comite´ Ouvrier Antijuif," or "Ligue Antijuive." In the XXI century, Catholic humanitarians speak the language of transnational institutions and are based in charities. But they also cultivate the fantasy of somehow removing Israel and its people.

There are Catholic bishops who claim that the Jewish State is "the new apartheid," and this blood libel has been embraced even by cardinals and bishops. But in the State of Israel all citizens – Jew and Arab – are equal before the law. Israel has no Population

[31] "Dutch MP calls to slash funding of anti-Israel NGOs," Jerusalem Post, June 27, 2011
[32] "Caritas Representative to Head UN NGO Conference," NGO Monitor Digest (Vol. 3 No. 7) March 15, 2005

Registration Act, no Group Areas Act, no Mixed Marriages and Immorality Act, no Separate Representation of Voters Act, no Separate Amenities Act, no pass laws or any of the myriad apartheid laws.

Israel is a vibrant democracy with a free press and an independent judiciary, and accords full political, religious and other human rights to all of its people, including its more than one million Arab citizens, many of whom hold positions of authority including cabinet ministers, members of parliament and judges at every level, including that of the Supreme Court. All citizens vote on the same roll in regular, multiparty elections; there are Arab parties and Arab members of other parties in Israel's parliament. Arabs and Jews share all public facilities, including hospitals and malls, buses, cinemas and parks.

According to the narrative offered by the Christian leaders, Arab and Muslim terrorism against Israel is a regrettable but understandable response to the Israeli "occupation" of the territories. This narrative is demonstrably flawed, as violence against Israelis and Jews in the region pre-dates the 1967 war by decades, and Israel returned to the Bible's areas inhabited by Jews for centuries. When Samuel Kobia, head of the World Council of Churches, declares Israel's occupation "a sin against God,"[33] the Christian leader theologically demonizes the Jewish people. The World Council of Churches contains all the major church bodies in the world and has a joint working group with the Vatican and all the mainline Protestant denominations—Presbyterians, Episcopalians, Methodists, Lutherans, and Congregationalists, as well as the National Council of Churches.

The Vatican ignores the fact that Israel is the only country in the region where Christian communities thrived in recent decades. The Arab Christian community maintains among the highest matriculation scores of any population; proportionally, Arab Christians also produce very high numbers of university graduates.

---

[33] "WCC Head Calls Israeli Occupation 'a sin against God'," Beliefnet, August 28, 2009

That is a mark of pride not only for the Christian community but for the State of Israel.

The Vatican has produced scant account of the trauma to which the second intifada has subjected Israeli civilians, and it has endorsed policies, such as the "right of return" of Palestinian refugees since 1948, that would spell the death of the Jewish state. But unfortunately, the Vatican stance against Israel is not unique.

The Church of England, leader of the Anglo Saxon Christianity, has also an anti-Israel position. The Episcopal Church, with 2 million members in the U.S., has provided support for anti-Israel activists. The Greek Orthodox Church, which is the largest private landowner in Israel, has been even more radically against Israel and the Jews. The Methodist Church of Britain, the fourth largest Christian denomination in the UK with 70 million members worldwide, voted to boycott Israeli-produced goods and services from the West Bank because of Israel's "illegal occupation of Palestinian lands." The 2.4-million-member Presbyterian Church voted to "initiate a process of phased selective divestment in multinational corporations operating in Israel." The United Church of Christ endorsed a range of economic leverages that included divestment.

In most of the global Christian forums, Israel is portrayed as a "colonialist oppressor," Palestinian national aspirations are celebrated, while Jewish aspirations are denigrated, and the wars waged by Arabs seeking to wipe out the Jewish state are characterized as "aggressive wars" provoked by Israel. No mention of suicide bombings or rockets, except possibly to justify them as understandable expressions of "rage." Catholic movements promote a retrograde anti-Jewish theology of supersession that has long since been repudiated by mainstream Christian denominations and uses rhetoric ("Jesus is on the cross again with thousands of crucified Palestinians around him") that can only serve to inflame anti-Jewish prejudice. There are many influential organizations, publications and schools of thought which brand themselves "Christian" or moral but which condemn and vilify Israel.

Palestinian Christians have long been among Israel's most vocal critics, using every opportunity to portray the Jewish State as a malevolent force and to downplay the religious-messianic component of the Islamic war against Israel.

I don't really believe that Catholicism has changed its spots and put 1,700 years of anti-Semitism behind it. If it were true that Christendom has changed then Churches and Christian organizations all over the world would be uniting to condemn the terrorists who are trying to take away Jewish lives. It would support the right for Israel to live in peace, which means using the force to break the terrorists and keep order in the land in which the Jews live. They would recognize the Jews' right to live in the land of the Bible.

Christendom remains the largest faith organization in the world with 2.1 billion people (the next largest being Islam with 1.5 billion). The Christian West has authority and power concerning Israel's existence and survival. It must act now to condemn the appeasement of Israel's enemies and to recognize that Israel is essential for the future of freedom in the Middle East. The Pope must immediately address the racist claim that Israel is an "apartheid state." This claim is also both ludicrous and dangerous. The claim is a vicious lie and, given the Church's commitment to anti-racism, it is fitting for the Pope to expose the lie for what it is.

Israel's position in the Middle East can be compared to the Jewish life in the Middle Ages. During the dark ages, Christians said Jews had no right to live among them as Jews. They should convert. Then the Christian princes of Europe (with Martin Luther and the Popes' help) said Jews had no right to live among them. Ghettos were formed. Then Hitler said Jews have no right to live. The existence of Israel should have positive theological significance because of the existence of the Jews as a people. Israel's existence as a people is a gift to the Gentile community of nations.[34] The permanence of Israel is part of God's design to

---

[34] "What the Pope should say" by David Weinberg, Jerusalem Post, March 19, 2000

~ 21 ~

enrich the world, to make it a better place for His children. The establishment, survival, and advancement of the State of Israel are more than political or secular events. Israel stands as vindication of the Biblical spirit and values and as an example of how a diverse population lives under God and within the framework of Justice in a liberal democracy.

Unfortunately, Israel's situation in 2013 is similar to Czechoslovakia's in 1938. A young vibrant state, the only liberal democracy in Eastern Europe, Czechoslovakia had Skoda, one of the world's largest military complexes. The Nazi neighbor demanded the annexation of the Sudeten region, settled by three million Germans. But the Sudeten mountains, like Israel's Judea and Samaria, were the only position from which the Bohemian plain, with the capital, Prague, was defensible. Hitler's demand was "Land for Peace." Neville Chamberlain, the cowardly British diplomat, flew to Munich, where the Sudetenland was given to Hitler. He returned with a piece of paper bearing Hitler's signature and "peace for our time." Chamberlain sold out the brave Czech democracy to "Herr Hitler," as Winston Churchill called him. When Czechoslovakia was a flourishing democracy, the Jews in Palestine were busy laying the foundation stones of their state. They based their claim to the land of their fathers on the Balfour Declaration, which promised, in the name of the British Empire, to permit the Jews to once again build their national home in the land of Israel from the Mediterranean to the Jordan river. But in the period 1938-39, instead of dealing with Hitler's death cult, His Majesty's government was busy preparing the infamous "White Paper," intended to appease the Arabs by restricting Jewish immigration. This decision was taken by the British cabinet headed by Chamberlain, the same who had sold out Czechoslovakia to Hitler. The Vatican then supported the White Paper.

Israel now, Czechoslovakia then; both young democracies ridden with minority problems; both protected by an industrial-military complex; both defendable from a mountain range situated close to the would-be enemy. There, it was the Sudetenland; in Israel, it is Judea-Samaria.

If Czechoslovakia was described as an "appendix" which must be excised, in Europe's hate speech It is the "settlements." If the Nazis shouted "today we have Germany, tomorrow the whole world," in current Euro-Arab coinage it is "from the Green Line today to the 'Blue {Mediterranean} Line' tomorrow."

Even from a military point of view the situation is very similar. Hitler had no heavy guns to crack the Sudeten fortifications, and was unprepared for an all-out war. But he just needed a "Regional Conference" in Munich. The participants were Germany, Italy, France, Britain, and, of course, Czechoslovakia, whose delegates waited outside, Hitler having refused to let them in. Nothing has changed in the last twenty years: Europe, the Arab states and their Palestinian clients are aiming to create a state west of the Jordan as a springboard from which to eliminate the Jewish énclave; the Americans are just guarding their interests without "offending anyone," while the Europeans are preserving their Arab-Islamic oil, whatever the cost to a Jewish Israel that is stubbornly insisting on preventing a Palestinian state and assuring its survival.

Like Hitler, the Arabs have learned how to exploit the much-admired European notion of national self determination as a means of extending their hegemony over all of Israel.

If Hitler's club was the threat of war, the Arabs' weapon is terrorism. The dark irony is that the Europeans who are supporting the Palestinians' "right of return" are living in homes stolen from Jews they helped to gas.

In 1939, the Nazis entered Prague without firing a shot.

Czechoslovakia was wiped off the map. In the end, Hitler was beaten, but 50 to 60 million "victims of peace" were no more. If in the wartime period the Vatican had taken a moral stand against Nazism, the outcome might have been different for the Jewish people. But that was 1942. By 2012, the Church should know better. Yet it seems that as was the case in World War II, the Vatican is again pursuing a joint cause with evil forces to buy temporary security. After Hitler's Final Solution, which tried to destroy the body of the Jewish people, and Stalin's war on

Zionism, which tried to destroy the heart of the Jewish people, it's now the turn of the Palestinian fabrication seeking to destroy the history of the Jewish people.

This book seeks to answer a tragic question: Will the Vatican be compelled to sacrifice again the people of Israel when the knife descends on Isaac? A century ago Europe was the center of Jewish life. More than 80 percent of world Jewry lived there. The Holocaust pulverized that Jewish existence. In the near future, the same percentage of world Jewry will live in the State of Israel. That is why the Vatican's stance on the Jewish State is the only measure of whether the Church is really serious about atoning for its sins against the Jewish people. Is there a connection between the Vatican's silence when Jews were being killed in Europe and its anti-Israel policy now that Jews have finally rebuilt their state, after 2,000 years of exile and bloodbath?7

In 2013, the College of Cardinals elected a man committed to the Catholic-Jewish relations, Cardinal Jorge Mario Bergoglio, known as Pope Francis. As archbishop of Buenos Aires, Bergoglio had celebrated Rosh Hashanah and Hanukkah in synagogues, voiced solidarity with Jewish victims of Iranian terrorism and co-written a book with a rabbi, Avraham Skorka. He also attended a commemoration of Kristallnacht, the wave of Nazi attacks against Jews in November 1938. But will Pope Francis work with and for Israel's Jews? One of the grave dangers in the Vatican's dialogue with Judaism has been the Catholic Church's attempt to drive a wedge between the "good" and docile Jews of the Diaspora and the "bad" and arrogant Jews of Israel.

Forty years ago, Jorge Mario Bergoglio made an unfortunately timed first visit to Israel. It was early October 1973, and Bergoglio had been in Rome completing a course for his job as the Provincial Superior of the Society of Jesus in Argentina. The future Pope flew to Israel intending to tour widely, but arrived at the very start of the Yom Kippur War. Because of the fighting, Bergoglio was unable to tour and spent six days confined to the hotel. He then witnessed Israel's siege and existential struggle to survive. Let's hope that Pope Francis will be different from his predecessors and stand up for truth.

This book seeks to answer a tragic question: Will the Vatican be compelled to once again sacrifice the people of Israel when the knife descends upon Isaac? A century ago Europe was the center of Jewish life. More than 80 percent of world Jewry lived there. The Holocaust pulverized that Jewish existence. In the near future, the same percentage of world Jewry will live in the State of Israel. That is why the Vatican's stance on the Jewish State is the only measure of whether the Church is really serious about atoning for its sins against the Jewish people. Is there a connection between the Vatican's silence when Jews were being killed in Europe, and its anti-Israel policy now that Jews have finally rebuilt their state after 2,000 years of exile and bloodbath?

Giulio Meotti

2. No Promised Land, No Chosen People

From Nostra Aetate to the Synod

Catholicism had long viewed Judaism as a pariah faith, and the Jews a group destined to wander the earth for their complicity in the death of Jesus.[35] The historical "proof" of this proto-Holocaust theology, according to Christian thinkers, was evidenced by the first century destruction of Judea at the hand of the Romans, with the overthrow of the Jewish king, the fall of Jerusalem, the destruction of the holy Temple, and the perennial dispersal of the Jewish people. For the first 17 years of Israel's existence, from 1948 to 1965, the Vatican refused to recognize Israel for theological reasons:[36] the Jews had, the Church taught, killed Jesus, and to punish them, God had sentenced the Israelites to an eternity of wandering. The new Jewish homeland was, therefore, a blasphemous circumvention of God's curse. "Rejecters of Christ,"[37] their land has rejected them. Forever.

Jerusalem became the "Deicide City," and its fall was commemorated in the Catholic liturgy. Zionism is to be deprecated, because it endeavors to improve the divinely ordained condition of the Jews and it affirms the vibrancy of Jewish existence. The Church has displaced Israel forever. God has abandoned the Jews and they have been dismissed from the Revelation. Jewish history ended with the appearance of Christianity, and that Jews continue to exist thereafter is nothing

---

[35] "Antisemitism, The Longest Hatred" by Robert Wistrich, Pantheon Books, 1991
[36] "Closing the book of the dark past," Catholic Herald, July 29, 1983
[37] "Der Vatikan und Palestina" by H. F. Kock, Wien, 1973

more than a curiosity. The Church constituted "the New Israel." Jerusalem is no longer on earth, but in heaven.

This is the theology which formed the basis for the Church-spawned anti-Semitism of the past 1,700 years.[38] King Dagobert expelled the Jews from France (632-638); Henry II expelled the Jews from southeast Germany (1012); Pope Gregory VII prohibited Jews from holding office in Europe (1073); the first Crusade in Germany resulted in the killing of 12,000 Jews along the Rhine River (1096); Jews were driven out of Belgium (1121); Jews suffered a pogrom in Norwich, England (1144); the Church decreed that any Christians volunteering to fight in the Crusade would be released from all debts owed to Jews (1146); King Philip of France expelled the Jews, confiscated their property, turned synagogues into churches, and forced Jews to wear badges (1182); Pope Innocent III promoted the Fourth Crusade, demanding Christian rulers make Jews atone for the sin of "deicide" (1198-1216); the Fourth Lateran Council introduced the idea that European Jews wear badges (1215); King Louis IX demanded all Jews be baptized, and burned 24 cartloads of Talmud in Paris with the approval of Pope Gregory IX (1226-1274); Jews were forced to wear cone-shaped hats in addition to badges in Vienna (1267); King Edward I banished Jews from England, forcing 16,000 to leave (1290); Jews were accused of poisoning wells and causing the Black Death (1348-1350); Spanish Jews were forced to leave or be massacred (70 communities were destroyed, 1391); Jews in Vienna had possessions confiscated and children converted (1421); the Spanish Inquisition, under direction of the Roman Catholic Church, perpetrated against Jews torture, heavy fines, confiscation of property, banishment, and death (1483-1492); 300,000 Jews were expelled from Spain (1492); Martin Luther wrote a proto-Holocaust pamphlet entitled "The Jews and Their Lies"; Pope Clement VII banished Jews from the Vatican (1593); ghettos were established in Italy (1624); pogroms swept over southern Russia against the Jews, causing their emigration to the West (1881); and

---

[38] "The Popes against the Jews" by David Kertzer, Vintage, 2002

the list continues with the Holocaust cataclysm and the killing of one third of the world's Jews.

After the war, theologians were forced to face the fact that the Holocaust occurred in the heart of Christian Europe, and that Christianity had, at the very least, helped create the environment in which this massacre could take place. The historical challenge was to learn how this had happened. The cornerstone of Christian anti-Semitism has been this "displacement myth," which rings with the genocidal note. This is the myth that the mission of the Jewish people was finished with the coming of Jesus, that "the old Israel" was written off with the appearance of "the new Israel." "To teach that a people's mission in God's providence is finished, that they have been relegated to the limbo of history, has murderous implications which murderers will in time spell out."[39] This theology found its ultimate truth in the gas chambers.

In June 1943, while the Nazis were implementing the "Final Solution" of the Jewish question, Pope Pius XII reaffirmed the doctrine of supersession in his encyclical Mystici Corporis Christi, writing that "the New Testament took the place of the Old Law which had been abolished... this effected a transfer... from the Synagogue to the Church."[40] It was only in 1965 that the Church in the Nostra Aetate declaration of Vatican II modified this horrible doctrine. But it opened the door to another theological conundrum.

Pope John XXIII charged Cardinal Augustin Bea, president of the Secretariat for Christian Unity of the Holy See, with the task of preparing a draft on the relationship between the Church and the Jewish people for the consideration of the Council Fathers.[41] However, European conservatives and Arab bishops rejected the draft proposal that unequivocally declared that "the Chosen People cannot without injustice be termed a deicidal race." So the Vatican reiterated its position against the Chosen: "Although the Church is

---

39 "The crucifixion of the Jews" by Franklin Littell, Mercer University Press, 2000
40 "A moral reckoning" by Daniel Goldhagen, Vintage, 2003
41 "Storia del Concilio Vaticano II" by Giuseppe Alberigo, Il Mulino, 1999

the new people of God, the Jews should not be presented as repudiated or cursed by God."

Writing in the September 1964 issue of "The Jewish Horizon,"[42] the literary organ of the Religious Zionists of America, Rabbi Joseph B. Soloveitchik, leader of Orthodox Judaism in the United States, published a letter on the developments that had transpired between the Church and the Jews during the Vatican Council. "They should say chatanu (we have sinned) for rushing in where angels fear to tread," Soloveitchik wrote in reference to those Jews who had participated in dialogue with the Church. The Jewish sage was furious over the disappearance of the term "deicide" in the final draft and on the Vatican refusal to recognize the existence of the State of Israel.[43]

Not until Vatican Council II did the Catholic Church commence a reconciliation with the Jewish people. In 1965, the Council asserted the Jews' common heritage with Catholics, the Jews' lack of collective guilt for the death of Christ, Israel's freedom from God's curse, and the special loving relationship between Catholics and Jews. But Nostra Aetate did not ask forgiveness from the Jews for the Church's past Anti-Semitism nor did it assert the contemporary validity of Judaism. Nor did the Council assert the existence of the State of Israel.

The "moderated" Nostra Aetate eliminated the denial of Jews' collective responsibility for the death of Jesus and omitted regret for the expression "guilty of deicide."[44] It no longer "condemned" (damat) anti-Semitism, but it merely "deplored" (deplorat) it. The Council's declaration added also a statement of eschatological hope for the union of Israel and the Church. This last statement is the reaffirmation of the Christian mission to the Jews.

---

[42] Joseph B. Soloveitchik in The Jewish Horizon, September-October, 1964

[43] "Revisiting Vatican II's theology of the people of God," by Elizabeth Groppe, Theological Studies, September 2011

[44] "The Church and the Jews: Struggle of Vatican II" by Judith Hershcopf, American Jewish Year Book, 1965

Rabbi Abraham Heschel called the draft "spiritual fratricide"[45] and declared that, faced with the choice of conversion or death in the gas chambers of Auschwitz, he would choose the second. "I'd rather go to Auschwitz than give up my religion." Heschel had an audience with Pope Paul VI[46] in order to persuade him to adopt the original language against the conversion of the Jews and the calumny of deicide. But he failed, since the Eastern churches, prominently represented in the Vatican Council, were opposed.

Maximos IV Saigh, patriarch of the Eastern-rite Melkites, was one of the champions on the progressive side at the council, but took an anti-Semitic stance. He declared he would walk out of the council hall if the charge of deicide against the Jews was withdrawn. Pope Paul VI told his associates that if the patriarch took so drastic a step, then, as Pope, he would have no option but to close down the discussion. But more important than the deicidal question, Nostra Aetate, which was later presented as the Magna Carta of the Jewish-Christian rapprochement, made no mention of the State of Israel. During that period, there was a growing sense in the Church of the relationship between the Gospel and issues of "justice and peace" reflected in a range of papal encyclicals ("Mater et Magistra and Pacem in Terris" of John XXIII, "Populorum Progressio and Evangelii Nuntiandi" of Paul VI, and later "Redemptoris Hominis and Laborem Exercens" of John Paul II). Translated to the Middle East, two conflicting tendencies were developing: theological respect for the Jews and political support for the Arabs.

The choice made by the Church during the Vatican Council had tragic consequences in the Middle East. The Vatican became hostage of anti-Zionism. The Nostra Aetate was followed by the "Guidelines and Suggestions for Implementing the Conciliar Declaration Nostra Aetate" (1974) and the "Notes on the Correct Way to Present the Jews and Judaism in Preaching and Catechesis

---

[45] "The Human and the Holy" by Donald Moore, Fordham, 1989
[46] "The Emergence of Jewish Theology in America" by Robert Goldy, Indiana University Press, 1990

in the Roman Catholic Church" (1985).[47] Why did the Catholic framers choose to ignore Israel, which after the Holocaust is the major Jewish question relevant for Western civilization? Were the bishops aware of the religious significance which the State of Israel holds for the Jewish people? Why was there no reference made to the State of Israel nine years later in the "Guidelines"? Why did it take twenty years for the Vatican to merely mention the word "Israel" in the "Notes" of 1985?

Then chief rabbi of Paris, Meyer Jais, wrote: "Jews are unanimous in interpreting the complete silence of the Council's Declaration and of the Roman document on the historical and religious bonds between the Jewish people and the Holy Land as proof of the total absence of any significant change in the Church's new outlook on Judaism."[48]

"The existence of the State of Israel and its political options should be envisaged not in a perspective which is in itself religious, but in their reference to the common principles of international law," says the important "Notes." The Nostra Aetate, instead of being a turning point in the Christian-Jewish relations, has been a tragedy which separated the inseparable: the deity, the people, and the land of Israel.

It is the most dramatic theological decision made by the Vatican after the Holocaust. It affected the future relations with the State of Israel. For the Vatican, Israel is not the heir of the Biblical people but a truncated, non-Jewish temporary state. Voices opposed to Catholic-Jewish rapprochement were heard at the early stage from two major sources which were to continue massive efforts to prevent Council action: the Arab nations and the ultra-conservative officials of the Curia. Gamal Abdul Nasser's "Voice of the Arabs" broadcast on November 7, 1963 that there was "a world Zionist plot to capitalize on the Vatican Council to further the oppression of the Palestinian refugees."[49] Theological

---

[47] "Catholics, Jews and the State of Israel" by Anthony Kenny, Paulist, 1993
[48] See Kenny
[49] "Let us prove strong: the American Jewish Committee" by Marianne Rachel Sanua

opposition from conservative sources was reflected in an article by Giacomo Lauri Volpi which appeared in L'Osservatore Romano (the official Vatican paper) on March 8, 1961, describing the Roman emperor Titus, who destroyed the Second Temple, as possibly the "executor of a supernatural will,"[50] who knew that the "Jewish people had stained themselves with a horrible crime deserving of expiation." Every prelate found in his box a 900-page volume titled "The Plot Against the Church," filled with the most primitive anti-Semitism. No one knew how the book was distributed to the Council Fathers (someone said Egypt), and it produced little effect other than indignation. But it did show to which lengths the opposition was prepared to go.

Another pamphlet distributed at a Franciscan sanctuary near Rome, written by someone calling himself Fra Giorgio da Terni, charged: "All of the most famous popes, saints and fathers of the Church have... warned against the epidemic Jewish disease, more contagious than the plague or venereal disease... Go and ask the Arabs who the Jews are, and you will really learn how they hate Jesus." The same poison oozed from letters written by Fr. Luigi Macali, a moral theologian at the Pontifical Theological University of St. Bonaventure in Rome, to Bishop Luigi Carli of Segni. Macali alleged that from the beginning "all the evils, all the persecutions of the church have come from the synagogues."[51] But today, he wrote, the Church "has come to the point of indicting itself while gaily absolving its oldest and most deadly enemy."

Another anti-Semitic publication was privately distributed to the Council Fathers, "The Jews and the Council in the Light of Scripture and Tradition," by a pseudonymous Bernardus, who cited Catholic sources supporting the deicide charge against Jews, proclaimed that Jews could only wipe out the curse upon them by converting to Christianity.

---

[50] "The Church and the Jews" by Judith Hershcopf
[51] "The beginning of the beginning" by John Wilkins, Commonweal Magazine, January 18, 2008

Patriarch Kyrillos VI of Alexandria, head of the Coptic Orthodox Church in Egypt, branded the Council's preliminary approval of the declaration "an imperialistic plot that has nothing to do with religion"[52] and went on to say, "The Holy Bible convicted the Jews and their children of Christ's crucifixion and to absolve them of that crime would be open to refutation of the Bible." The Nostra Aetate didn't challenge or affect Arab Christianity's hatred for the Jews.

In Jordan, the churches called to say their prayers at home in Arabic "in order to force the Vatican to cancel its decision absolving Jews," and sent a cable to the Pope asking that the declaration be dropped from the Council. A Syrian government bulletin reported that Chaldean-Rite Bishop Stephane Bello of Aleppo has dispatched "tens of telegrams" to the Vatican in protest. Despite repeated assurances from Cardinal Bea and others that the purpose of the declaration was "purely religious," Arab leaders continue to claim it to be Zionist-inspired and part of a plot "to mobilize world Catholic opinion against the Arabs for reigniting the Palestinian question," in the words of Syrian Premier Salah el Bitar. A Syrian government radio broadcast declared, "When the Jews dipped their hands into the innocent blood of Jesus Christ they were in fact trying to assassinate Christ's principles and teachings."

After the Second Vatican Council, anti-Jewish ugly themes kept resurfacing through bishops and churches: that the Jews were "killers of God," doomed to eternal servitude for the crime of "deicide," a crime that could only be expiated by their conversion; or that the Jews were conspirators against the Church. A cable was sent to Pope Paul, with copies to the seven Oriental Rite cardinals at the Ecumenical Council, reminding the pontiff of his pilgrimage to the Holy Land and "the results of Jewish crimes against Palestine's Arabs." Recalling the intensity of these diplomatic and ecclesiastical initiatives, we may count ourselves fortunate that

---

[52] "Israel Yearbook on Human Rights" by Yoram Dinstein, Volume 6, 1976

Nostra Aetate was promulgated. But since then, two conflicting Vatican tendencies were developing and are still dominating: theological dialogue with Judaism, and political support for the Arabs.

In Bea's speeches during the draft's elaboration, he portrayed the State of Israel as a pure political reality.[53] Bea, who played a central role in the development, passage and implementation of Nostra Aetate, believed that the declaration treated Judaism, or as he called it, "the Mosaic religion," as a merely religious phenomenon. "The schema treats exclusively of a pure religious question," "we are treating a mere religious question," "the question is purely religious." For Bea, and thus for the Vatican, the return of the Jews to their homeland and the rebirth of the Jewish nation held no religious significance. Replacement theology stated that Christians had inherited the covenant and replaced the Jews as the chosen people. The concept of replacement geography similarly replaces the historical connection of one people to the land with a connection between another people and the land.

A year later, the Vatican Council published a work by Cardinal Bea entitled "The Church and the Jewish People".[54] Bea fell into the use of language reminiscent of wandering theology which had set in motion the Holocaust. "The fate of Jerusalem," Bea tells us, "constitutes a sort of final reckoning at the end of a thousand years of infidelities and opposition to God." According to Bea, Jews and Judaism existed merely as a "witness to their iniquity and to the truth of the Christian faith." It is understandable, therefore, according to Bea, why Christian bodies reacted to the re-establishment of the modern State of Israel in 1948 with outright opposition and demonization.

The Vatican Council's silence on Israel would have severe consequences on the Church's relations with the Jews. When in 1986 Pope John Paul II went to the main synagogue in Rome, it was the first time in 2,000 years a Pope had set foot in a Jewish

---

[53] "Catholics, Jews and the State of Israel" by Anthony Kenny, Paulist, 1993
[54] "The Church and the Jewish People" by Augustin Bea, Harper and Row, 1966

temple. It was a gesture of friendship. But the most important issue was missing from the Pope's speech. There was not a word about the State of Israel.

As Pulitzer Prize winner Charles Krauthammer wrote, "Such speech could have been given, say, in 1936."[55] Classic anti-Semitism is not the biggest threat to Jewish existence. The Pope knew that the biggest threat to Jewish life after Auschwitz was the threat to Israel. But he chose to not mention it. Why? The Pope in the synagogue treated the Jews as merely a religious community when in fact they are a people. To address the Jews purely as a religious community it means denying their peoplehood. It means denying them a place among the nations.

Catholicism is now entering the post-post Nostra Aetate age. The generation that was shaped by the Vatican II is passing from the scene. But its legacy lives on with the exclusion of the State of Israel from the family of nations. Catholicism refused to acknowledge Israel's existence to contemporary Judaism.

The Vatican's hostility to Zionism and Jewish sovereignty had been prominently displayed in October 2010, when the Holy See gathered dozens of bishops for a synod in Rome. During this unprecedented Vatican "Special Assembly for the Middle East," 172 Catholic bishops from Islamic countries, 14 Vatican officials, 14 non-Catholic Christians and 30 academic experts spent two weeks discussing the future of Catholic communities in the Middle East. According to the British columnist Melanie Phillips, "the Vatican reversed into a darker age,"[56] while Ephraim Zuroff, director of the Simon Wiesenthal Center in Israel and famous Nazi hunter, declared that "once again we have become Christianity's scapegoat."[57]

The Vatican's synod reopened the wounds of the Wandering Jew malediction, which caught the imaginations of Christians for

[55] "The Pope and the Jews" by Charles Krauthammer, The Washington Post, April 13, 1986
[56] The Spectator, October 26, 2010
[57] Arutz Sheva, January 21, 2010

centuries as the symbol of God's rejection of the Jewish people. Condemned to homelessness, the Wandering Jew personified the nation responsible for the Crucifixion. Early Christian theologians similarly taught that descendants of Abraham lost all rights to the covenants and blessings for having denied Jesus. According to this model, the destruction of the Second Temple and the failure of the Bar Kochba revolt confirmed divine retribution for Jewish misdeeds. The Nazis modernized the Wandering Jew image into a propaganda tool. Joseph Goebbels, Nazi Germany's minister of propaganda, released a film in 1940 titled "Der ewige Jude," the Eternal Jew. The film aimed to portray the Jews as wandering parasites, a disgusting and inferior race, microbes, and dirty creatures. The opening scene shows a rat pack coming up from a sewer juxtaposed with a crowd of Jews on a busy Polish street.

The State of Israel posed an urgent dilemma to the anti-Semitic impulse of some Christian thinking. According to the rejection theory of Jewish exile, the land rights and promises to the Hebrew people were no longer applicable to the Jews. But how does one explain the miraculous rebirth of the Jewish state? This culture of hate and gross misunderstanding of Scripture almost destroyed the Christian Church. The horrors of the Holocaust allowed Christians to see the fruit of a theology that deemed Jews irrelevant at best. Now the survival of the Jewish people after nearly 2,000 years of exile could be appreciated as a true miracle not something offensive to Christianity but rather a miracle that reaffirms our faith in God. During the synod in 2010, the Vatican chose another theology — that of demonization.

Years ago, the Soviet dissident Natan Sharansky proposed "the three-D test" for determining whether what purports to be criticism of Israeli policy is in fact tainted with deeply rooted antipathy to Jews, or anti-Semitism. Sharansky's three Ds were de-legitimization, demonization and double-standards. A 40-page Vatican document, which formed the basis for the synod, castigated what it terms "the Israeli occupation of Palestinian territories" as a "political injustice imposed on the Palestinians."[58] The language of the Vatican smacks of Sharansky's Ds.

Accusing Israel of stifling Palestinian daily life, without mention of the terrorist attacks that made Israeli restrictions inevitable, paints the Jews as tyrannical. This is demonization. Demonization is also an appropriate criticism of the words of Catholic intellectuals such as Vittorio Messori, the leading Italian Catholic journalist who first interviewed Pope John Paul II. After the synod, Messori indicted Israel as the main element responsible for Christian persecution in the Islamic lands. "What happened so far? Every government of the Islamic nations is under the tsunami of the violent intrusion of Zionism."[59] But the Arab/Israeli conflict is not a struggle against apartheid or occupation, as Messori and other anti-Zionist Catholic intellectuals are claiming. It is a war against the Jewish people.

"The Holy Scriptures cannot be used to justify the return of Jews to Israel and the displacement of the Palestinians, to justify the occupation by Israel of Palestinian lands,"[60] proclaimed Monsignor Cyril Salim Bustros, Greek Melkite archbishop of Our Lady of the Annunciation in Boston and president of the "Commission for the Message" of the synod. "We Christians cannot speak of the 'promised land' as an exclusive right for a privileged Jewish people. This promise was nullified by Christ."

"As a Christian, and especially as a Middle-Eastern Christian—and this is the unanimous opinion of the Middle-Eastern Christians, Catholics, Orthodox and Protestants—I see that the concept of the Promised Land cannot be used for the justification of the return of Jews to Israel and the displacement of Palestinians," Bustros went on to say. "The creation of the State of Israel in 1948—after the UN resolution in 1947 regarding the partition of Palestine which was under the British mandate between Arab and Jews—is a political issue not a religious one. It

---

58 "The Vatican and the 3Ds," The Jerusalem Post, June 3, 2010
59 Il Corriere della Sera, January 7, 2011
60 The Jerusalem Post, October 23, 2010

is a fact of history like other facts. Jews who were persecuted in Europe and suffered the horrors of the Shoah decided to come to Palestine and build, with the Jews who were there, a country for their own. They could have chosen another place. But they chose Palestine, some of them relying on the theme of the Promised Land, and others only because of the memory of the Jews who lived there 2000 years ago. So they came in great numbers; a war arose between them and the Arabs living there, and they won the war; hundreds of thousands of Palestinians were forced to leave their homes and flee to surrounding Arabic countries such as Lebanon, Syria and Jordan. If some of the Jews based their return on the Old Testament theme of the Promised Land, this does not mean that God is behind their return and their victory against the Arabs. It is a religious interpretation of an historical event."

About Jewish chosenness, Bustros was also clear: "As for the idea of the chosen people, it is clear, according to Christian theology and especially to St. Paul, that after Christ there is no longer one particular chosen people." It is the same bishop who gave this explanation to a US journalist in Lebanon about the cooperation between Christians and Hezbollah's terror group: "When I speak with them, I claim the support to the liberation of Lebanon, we have a common enemy."[61]

The attack on Israel by Archbishop Bustros was not a single incident, but was reinforced in the official final message of the synod, which, under the heading "Cooperation and Dialogue with the Jews," argues that "recourse to theological and biblical positions, which use the Word of God to wrongly justify injustices, is not acceptable." It means that Israel cannot claim any theological and biblical attachment to the land. The Vatican de facto abolished Israel's sovereignty. Jesuit Father and theologian Francesco Rossi de Gasperis of the Pontifical Biblical Institute of Jerusalem once called it "theological negation of the people of Israel, a kind of cultural and spiritual Shoah, not dissimilar to what

---

[61] The Baltimore Sun, April 27, 1996

was seen in the churches of Europe during the age of Christendom."[62]

Reading Bustros' words, we should remember that there is not a single Church document — Catholic or mainline Protestant — that denounces or criticizes Palestinian Christianity's anti-Zionism. In private talks, some officials in the Vatican do state their personal regret at Palestinian anti-Zionism and neo-Marcionism. But nothing is said publicly, where most of the Catholic Middle Eastern bishops and officials support the new anti-Semitic theology. The reason Bustros said the Jews have no right to their own country is not political but theological, because he denies that the Jews are the "chosen people"; the bishop claims that this designation has been nullified by Christ, thus making all people chosen. It is a resurrection of the ancient Christian calumny that the Jews are damned for all time as cosmic exiles on account of their refusal to accept the divinity of Christ. It is therefore a profoundly anti-Jewish statement. In one fell swoop, a senior Church official sought to deny the unique, covenantal relationship between God and the Jews, rejecting the divine promise to restore the people of Israel to their Land.

In 2012 the Latin Patriarch of Jerusalem, Fouad Twal, declared that "Israel has nothing to do with the Bible."[63] Iraq's Archbishop, Louis Sako, asked to "separate between Judaism and Zionism."[64] Both have been important speakers at that synod. The malignant use of the expression "chosen Jews" is recurring in most of the attacks against Israel. Such vilification inspired historical waves of violence, like the pogroms, the expulsion of the Spanish Jews and Martin Luther's demonology (the founder of Protestantism argued that the Jews were no longer the chosen people but instead "the Devil's people"). "Modern-day Jews are not God's chosen people," the late head of Egypt's Coptic Orthodox Church, Pope Shenouda III, declared in a meeting with former US President

---

[62] Chiesa Espresso, March 27, 2002
[63] Yedioth Ahronoth, March 21, 2012
[64] Asia News, September 26, 2009

Jimmy Carter. "Do not believe their claim that they are God's chosen people, because it is not true."[65] It is no longer only Syria that aired a movie against the "Chosen Jews," or the former prime minister of Malaysia, Mohammad Mahathir, who warned that "the Jews must never think they are the chosen people." The obsession for this issue now widely appears in the latest indictments of Israel as an "apartheid state" and in the legal campaigns against the Law of Return. Elias Chacour, the Vatican-approved Catholic Archbishop of Israel, says that "we do not believe anymore that the Jews are the Chosen People."[66] Many anti-Semitic comments are based on the concept of Jews as the chosen people.

The hatred for the Jewish chosen-ness is the driving force behind anti-Semitism. "We are God's people," Hitler declared. He regarded the Jews as an obstacle to Aryan chose-ness. As he put it, "there cannot be two chosen peoples." Christian and Islamic anti-Semitism are related to the contention that they have replaced the Jews as the Chosen People. Acclaimed Greek composer Mikis Theodorakis told an interviewer that "today it is possible to say that this small nation is the root of all evil; it is full of self-importance and evil stubbornness."[67] Asked by his interlocutor, "What is it that holds us Jews together?" Theodorakis replied, "It is the feeling that you are the children of God. That you are the chosen." Jostein Gaarder, author of the literary bestseller Sophie's World, published an op-ed titled "God's Chosen People"[68] in the Aftenposten, one of Norway's major newspapers, in which he declared that Israel has lost its right to exist. "We no longer recognize the state of Israel... We don't believe in the idea of God's chosen people... To present oneself as God's chosen people is not just stupid and arrogant, but a crime against humanity. We call it racism." José Saramago, the Portuguese writer and Nobel Prize laureate, described the Jews in perfervid terms as

---

[65] "Pope Shenouda: Modern-day Jews not 'God's chosen people'," Egypt Independent, September 29, 2011

[66] "Holy Land, Hollow Jubilee" by Naim Ateek, Melisende, 1999

[67] "Choseness and its enemies" by Jon Levenson, Commentary, December 2008

[68] "Guds utvalgte folk" by Jostein Gaarder, Aftenposten, August 5, 2006

"contaminated by the monstrous and rooted 'certitude' that in this catastrophic and absurd world there exists a people chosen by God and that, consequently, all the actions of an obsessive, psychological, and pathological exclusivist racism are justified."[69]

This is the same delusional lexicon of medieval Jew-hatred. Taken to its logical end, this language suggests that there is only one price the Jews can pay for being accepted by the world: Israel's elimination. Indeed, this worldwide viewpoint condemns the Jews to homelessness and humiliation, chosen to walk the earth alone until the end of the days.

After the Lebanese-born Bustros' remarks caused a furor, the Vatican spokesman waited two days before issuing a mealy-mouthed statement which did little to calm the storm. "If one wants a summary of the synod's position, attention must currently be paid to the 'Message,' which is the only written text approved by the synod in the last few days," the Vatican's press director Father Federico Lombardi said. "There is also a great richness and variety in the contributions made by the fathers, but which as such should not all be considered as the voice of the synod as a whole."[70] Despite Lombardi's efforts to contain the fallout, that convocation of bishops was called by the Pope himself and the Vatican had officially delegitimized Israel while assaulting Judaism itself. The synod will be remembered as one of the most horrible moments of Vatican anti-Semitism in church history.

Bustros and his colleagues shamefully did not hesitate to invoke the sacred for their most profane of goals. Given the Catholic Church's long history of anti-Jewish persecution, it was incumbent upon Pope Benedict to transform this new turn of events into a profound opportunity to atone for what the Church has done to the Jewish people through the centuries.

Most important is that Bustros' claims against Israel were not unique at the Vatican synod. On October 14, Maronite archbishop

---

[69] "The world turned upside down" by Melanie Phillips, Encounter, 2010
[70] "Vatican Aide: "Voice" of Synod Is Final Message," Zenit, October 25, 2010

Edmond Farhat – former apostolic nuncio and the official representative of Vatican politics in Lebanon — spoke also at the synod.[71] And the judgments he expressed confirmed that for the Vatican the assumption still applies that the ultimate cause of all of the evils in the Middle East is precisely that "foreign body" which is Israel. Nuncio Farhat said, "The Middle Eastern situation today is like a living organ that has been subject to a graft it cannot assimilate and which has no specialists capable of healing it."[72] The Nazi ideologues could not have said it better. The Pope's October 25 homily at the close of the Synod would have been the good time to defend the presence of Israel in the family of the nations. The Pope did not take the opportunity to do so. That is why late Fr. Richard John Neuhaus, one of the major Catholic US intellectuals, wisely argued that the Election of Israel should have been incorporated in the Catechism of the Catholic Church.[73]

Speaking to Italian public television, the former Jerusalem patriarch, Michel Sabbah, during the synod declared that "we have the duty to resist to Israel."[74] The Vatican official then said that Israel was committing ethnic cleansing. "Israel would have all of Palestine without the Palestinians." His successor at the leadership of the Latin community in Israel, the patriarch Fouad Twal, added that the solution can be "one binational state,"[75] a naïve and violent idea used to undermine the Jewishness of Israel.

For the first time the "Instrumentum Laboris," the official Vatican document for the Synod, also denounced the "Israeli occupation," while the secretary of the Synod, Egyptian cardinal Antonios Naguib, during the Vatican assembly, equated terrorism and Israeli occupation, saying that the Israeli policies favor Islamic

---

[71] "Synodus Episcolorum Bulletin," Holy See Press Office
[72] "Intervention of Mons. Edmond Farhat, Titular Archbishop of Byblus, Apostolic Nuncio," Radio Vaticana, October 16, 2010
[73] "Salvation is from the Jews" by Richard John Neuhaus, First Things, November 2001
[74] Ansa News Agency, October 19, 2010
[75] Ansa News Agency, October 15, 2010

fundamentalism.[76] Twal said also that "a democratic state can't be also Jewish; you can't have both democracy and Zionism."

At the Synod, Elias Chacour, Catholic Archbishop of Nazareth and Galilee, also affirmed, "Where Israel was sixty years ago? How it started to exist suddenly? It happened a real ethnic cleansing of the Palestinians."[77] The major Vatican officials used a hateful propaganda to attack Israel. Chacour, the most influential Catholic Archbishop in Israel, also approved the replacement theology, when he wrote that "we have been taught for centuries that the Jews are the Chosen People. We do not believe anymore that they are the Chosen People of God, since now we have a new understanding of that Chosen-ness."[78]

Chacour was a major protagonist of the synod. He is also the deputy president of the Sabeel Ecumenical Liberation Theology Center, headquartered in Jerusalem, and a persistent source of anti-Zionist agitation. Since the Six Day War, a number of Arab Christians have downplayed Muslim and Arab hostility toward Jews and depicted Israel as a colonialist outpost in the Middle East. These polemicists include the gunrunning Melkite archbishop Hilarion Capucci, the late Edward Said, Latin patriarch Sabbah, and Anglican bishop Riah Hanna Abu El-Assal — all of whom have their admirers in the West.

Naim Ateek is the founder of Sabeel. The known Anglican priest portrays the Palestinians as Christ-like sufferers crucified by Israel. The movement's eschatology is that of Jewish repentance and abandonment of sovereignty leading to peace in the Middle East. In April 2004, the 5th International Sabeel Conference was held at the Pontifical Institute Notre Dame Centre in Jerusalem. Conceived in 1884 as a center for French pilgrims, in 1978 Pope John Paul II established it as a Pontifical Institute and Ecumenical Centre. After experiencing decades of decline and total rejection by

[76] Ansa News Agency, October 18, 2010
[77] Adnkronos News Agency, November 15, 2010
(http://www.adnkronos.com/AKI/Italiano/Video/?vid=3.1.1099454695)
[78] "Holy Land Hollow Jubilee" by Naim Ateek, Melisende, 1999, p. 112

many denominations, Replacement Theology has resurfaced in the form of Palestinian Liberation Theology.

Writing in the Journal of Ecumenical Studies in 2004, Adam Gregerman observed that "liberation theologians" published by Sabeel "perpetuate some of the most unsavory and vicious images of the Jews as malevolent, antisocial, hostile to non-Jews... These critiques lead to a demonization of the Jews." In the summer of 2006, many Christian figures, including Ateek, published "The Jerusalem Declaration on Christian Zionism."[79] The statement was written by Latin Patriarch Michel Sabbah of Jerusalem and other local heads of Churches in Jerusalem. It is said that Christian Zionism provides "a worldview where the Gospel is identified with the ideology of empire, colonialism and militarism." In its extreme form, "it laces an emphasis on apocalyptic events leading to the end of history rather than living Christ's love and justice today." These Christians "categorically reject Christian Zionist doctrines as false teaching that corrupts the biblical message of love, justice and reconciliation."

Another protagonist of the Synod has been Father Samir Khalid Samir, a Jesuit of Arab origin who prominently advises Pope Benedict XVI on Islam. In his 111 "Questions on Islam," Samir attacked Israel as responsible for the Middle Eastern troubles. "The problem goes back to the creation of the state of Israel and the partition of Palestine in 1948, decided by the superpowers without taking into account the population already present in the (Holy) Land. There resides the real root of all the wars that followed. To repair a serious injustice committed in Europe against a third of the world Jewish population, Europe (supported by the superpowers) decided to commit a new injustice against the Palestinian population, who are innocent of the martyrdom of the Jews."[80] The facts tell a complete different story.

There were 600,000 Jews in Israel on the day of its founding; an additional 700,000 were expelled from Arab lands, where the Jews

---

[79] Zenit News Agency, August 30, 2006
[80] Chiesa Espresso, August 30, 2006

had lived for 2,000 years prior to the arrival of the Arabs. By expelling the Jews, the Arab countries created a population concentration in Israel that made possible the country's emergence as a regional superpower. The results were an exchange of populations of roughly equal numbers, Palestinians leaving the new State of Israel and Jewish refugees arriving from Arab countries.

Fr. Samir maintains in any case that the existence of Israel is today a matter of fact that cannot be rejected, independently of its original sin. This is also the official position of the Holy See, with the judgment that the Arabs are the victims, and the Israelis are the oppressors. Even Islamist terrorism is traced back to this basic cause.

The leader of the Greek Catholic Church, Gregorios III Laham, declared after the synod, that the terrorism against Christians in Arab countries is part of a "Zionist conspiracy."[81] The statement was made at an archdiocesan ceremony in Lebanon meant to emphasize interreligious coexistence. The Melkite Church is in "full communion" with the Vatican. Gregorios' demonizing and blatantly false claim represents classic scapegoating of Jews.

The "Kairos Palestine"[82] document was launched in Bethlehem on December 11, 2009 by a panel chaired by the former Catholic Patriarch of Jerusalem Sabbah, named by Pope John Paul II. The World Council of Churches was quick to disseminate it among Protestant churches. During the Vatican Synod on the Middle East in 2010, the anti-Semitic document was presented in a Vatican-owned building run by Pax Christi, Catholic Action and the Franciscan Custodian of the Holy Land. The document is meant to mobilize Catholic and Protestant communities and churches worldwide in a program of boycotts, divestment and de-legitimization directed at the State of Israel. It alludes to a similarly named document issued in South Africa years ago, thus deliberately comparing Israel with the regime of apartheid and

---

81 The National Review, December 13, 2010
82 For the English version of the document, see: http://www.kairospalestine.ps/sites/default/Documents/English.pdf

Zionism with South African Aryanism. It employs hateful language, such as declaring that "the military occupation of our land is a sin against God and humanity." The Kairos Document is similar to Hamas and Fatah "talking points" but wrapped in Christian packaging. Among the signatures in the document is the former spokesman of the Greek Orthodox Church in Jerusalem, Father Atalla Hanna.

In a lecture given in Abu-Dhabi on June 19, 2002, Hanna said: "The Church fully supports the resistance for the sake of liberation from Israel. Some freedom fighters adopt martyrdom or suicide bombings, while others opt for other measures... Don't expect us to keep a distance and watch. We are in the struggle whether it is martyrdom or any other means... The Muslims and the Christians are one and cannot be separated from the struggle for the liberation of Palestine. We are Palestinians and Arabs."[83]

In a January 19, 2003 sermon marking the Epiphany and the baptism of Jesus at a Greek Orthodox cathedral in Jerusalem, Hanna said, "Palestine is from the sea to the river. We refuse any concession on even a grain of the land of our precious homeland. Just as Ramallah, Gaza, Nablus, and Jenin are Palestinian cities, so are Haifa, Nazareth, Jaffa, Ramle, Lod, Beersheba, Safed, and other Palestinian cities. We have not relinquished and we will not relinquish our historic right, and we will not agree to any concession on these cities. These are Palestinian cities that were occupied in 1948." About any possible peace agreement, Hanna proclaimed that "peace cannot be made with Satan. Israel is the greatest Satan. The Palestinians' rights will be restored only by resistance. What was taken by force will be restored only by force..."

Hanna delivered similar statements during a rally held on Friday, January 17, 2003 in the square of the Church of the Holy Sepulchre in Jerusalem. Participating in the rally were Christian clerics, Palestinian Christian personalities, and local residents.

---

[83] MEMRI Special Dispatch Series – No. 405, July 30, 2002

Hanna, who was introduced as the official spokesman of the Orthodox Church in Jerusalem and Holy Lands, gave a speech on behalf of the clerics. He spoke out in praise of suicide attacks. "We declare publicly our blessing, support, and legitimization of the brave Palestinian resistance [carried out] by any means, including the brave Fidaiyin. The names of the Fidaiyin Shahids [the martyrs] will be inscribed in the history of our Palestinian and Arab people in holy white letters..."

The Greek Orthodox Patriarch of Jerusalem, Irineos I, has used even more virulent rhetoric than his former spokesman Hanna. Irineos wrote about the "sentiments of disgust and disrespect that all the Holy Sepulcher Fathers are feeling for the descendants of the crucifiers of our Lord Jesus Christ, actual crucifiers of your people, Zionists Jewish conquerors of the Holy Land of Palestine."[84] Irineos is the head of the largest and most wealthy church in the Middle East. He also expressed his anti-Israeli stance in a letter on patriarchate letterhead to Arafat during the 2002 siege of Bethlehem's Church of the Nativity, which began when Palestinian terrorists barricaded themselves inside. "We wish to assure you, Dear Mr. President, that the Greek Orthodox Patriarchate of Jerusalem and myself stand side by side with your people in this fight for freedom and justice... We pray to the Almighty God of Love to give you success and victory in this holy struggle, and also help to establish His peace in the Holy Land." These letters were made public by the Israeli daily Ma'ariv as part of a series of articles between December 2002 and January 2004 on Irineos' pro-Palestinian attitude.

The Catholic de-legitimization of Israel passes through the war on Jerusalem. The Temple Mount, the place where Avraham came to sacrifice his son to God, the site of the first and second Jewish Temples, where the Jewish people worshipped for hundreds of years and the focal point of every practicing Jew's prayers, is under assault from the Vatican, which promoted a pact with the PLO

---

[84] The Jerusalem Post, January 3, 2003

meant to exclude the Jews from the old city. For example the Vatican's former Archbishop in Jerusalem, Michel Sabbah, ran an appeal to the European Union and United States to "stop the Hebraization of Jerusalem." The new Latin Patriarch, Fouad Twal, took part in a meeting in London with Anglican Archbishop Rowan Williams of Canterbury, in which the Vatican envoy denounced the "more than 550,000 Israelis living in East Jerusalem and the West Bank" and "the demography of Jerusalem changing rapidly with the sacred space being threatened."

The Islamic-Christian Committee, the Palestinian institution waging the war on Jewish Jerusalem, was co-founded by the former Greek Orthodox Archbishop Hanna and sees the participation of Catholic leaders like Claudette Habesch, Secretary General of Caritas Jerusalem for the last 25 years, which is the most important Vatican's humanitarian arm in the world. The Christian-Islamic Committee has seen the participation of Sheikh Tamimi, the highest profile Islamic judge of the Palestinian Authority and a self-professed anti-Semite. In May 2000, Yasser Arafat met Islamic and Christian clergymen, led by Tamimi and Archimandrite Hanna at the presidential offices in Ramallah. A few weeks later, before the Camp David summit, Jerusalem's Christian patriarchs backed Palestinian sovereignty over Jerusalem. Among the clergymen, Diodoros I, patriarch of the Greek Orthodox Church, Torkom II, patriarch of the Armenian Orthodox Church and Catholic Patriarch Michel Sabbah. Officials from the Custody of the Holy Land, a Franciscan-Vatican order with special authority over Christian sites, were also present at the meeting.

PA's President Mahmoud Abbas is following Arafat's path. Speaking at the International Conference for Defense of Jerusalem in Doha, Qatar, Abbas said in February 2011 that "the Israeli occupation authorities are using the ugliest and most dangerous means to implement plans to erase and remove the Arab-Islamic and the Christian character of east Jerusalem."[85]

---

[85] "Netanyahu Slams Abbas' 'Contemptible' Doha Speech," Arutz Sheva, February 26, 2012

According to the Islamic-Christian Committee, the conference's purpose is to combat the "Judaization of Jerusalem."

There were many Christian figures attending the event, like Elias Awad of the Catholic Patriarchate of Jerusalem, Patriarch Gabi Hachem of the Catholic Liqa Center and Bishop Georgi Panossian, Primate of the Armenian Orthodox Church. The United Nations also sent several high profile officials, Robert Serry, UN Coordinator for the Middle East Peace Process, and Filippo Grandi, Commissioner General of UNRWA.

Abbas denied the Jewish history on Temple Mount by stating that Israel plans to destroy the Al Aqsa Mosque, a lie designed to incite Muslims to rise up against Jews. Recently, the World Council of Churches also incited against the "occupation," "settlements," and "Jewish rights" in Jerusalem. As historian Bat Ye'or explained, in a large number of documents going back to the 1970s, "the Organization of the Islamic Conference recommended cooperation with Churches in the fight against Israel."[86] This emerged from a conference held in Amman in 2004 as part of the Muslim-Christian dialogue. The official theme was the protection against Israel of Muslim and Christian holy places in Jerusalem. At the Amman conference, the speakers emphasized the importance of "Muslim-Christian solidarity" in the fight to seize al Quds and to drive Israel out of it. Their proposals included the adoption of the Muslim and Christian sites in Jerusalem by mosques, churches and monastery, and by Muslim and Christian institutions worldwide. "Promoting al Quds would be done through films, television, songs, and festivals, under the supervision of a special Muslim and Christian cell that would be working with all the appropriate means."

The 23rd of December, 1995, is the turning point for the Islamic-Christian alliance against the Jews in Jerusalem.[87] The Greek Orthodox patriarch of the holy land, Deodorus I, handed

[86] "Jerusalem or al Quds" by Bat Ye'or, Journal for the Study of Antisemitism vol.3, 2011
[87] "Custody of Jerusalem Churches handed to Arafat," Reuters, December 23, 1995

over the custody of Churches in Jerusalem to PLO leader Arafat. This was done in the presence of the Catholic, Anglican and Greek Orthodox archbishops. The patriarch declared: "I am the heir of Sophronius and I am handing the keys (to Christian holy sites in Jerusalem) to the heir of Omar Ibn al-Khattab."

Omar, the caliph who claimed Jerusalem from Byzantine rule in 638, gave then Patriarch Sophronius custody of Churches and a pledge to safeguard them. The move was meant to put Christian holy places under the custody of Arafat, a Muslim, and to strengthen the Arab-Islamic claim to Jerusalem as the capital of a Palestinian state.

Why did Arafat mention this 1,300-year-old story? He saw himself as conquering Jerusalem a second time in history for the Muslims. Any reference to Omar simply means, "Jerusalem must be Judenrein." The final goal of this Muslim-Christian dialogue is to erase any Jewish presence in the so called "holy basin," an alliance of the mosques and the sepulcher which will exclude the Jews from the Temple Mount. As the early Christians had left the Temple deliberately in ruin, it is now the turn of the Islamicized Mount. Will the Christian Churches be able to convince the European Union, the UN and the US to call Jerusalem "Al Quds"?

The Vatican-PLO agreement enables the eviction of the Jews from Jerusalem. This is a memorandum signed by Palestinian and Vatican officials in 2000 which repeated the Vatican call for an international mandate to preserve "the proper identity and sacred character" of Jerusalem.[88] The Catholic Church wants Israel to relinquish sovereignty at the Western Wall and the Temple Mount. This is the "Holy Basin" formula, which refers to the area of the "Noble Sanctuary," the Mount of Olives, Mount Zion and a variety of Christian holy sites which the administration of former U.S. President Bill Clinton already began to recommend be administered under a "special regime."

---

[88] "Basic agreement between the Vatican and the Palestine Liberation Organization" (2000)

The Vatican also wants some sovereignty over the "Hall of the Last Supper" on Mount Zion in Jerusalem, the place where Jesus broke bread and drank wine with his disciples on the eve of crucifixion. Cardinal Jean-Louis Tauran, head of the Vatican's Council for Interreligious Dialogue, asked to place the holy site under the Vatican authority. The problem is that the site is also King David's Tomb, a complex of buildings of some 100,000 square feet where David and Solomon, and Jewish kings of Judea, are buried. This is the very building where until the liberation of the Old City of Jerusalem in 1967, people migrated to pray as it was the closest location to the Western Wall. David Ben-Gurion planted trees in its ancient courtyard. The Vatican would like to "Christianize" the holy site, like when a Catholic convent was built in Auschwitz. The Diaspora Yeshiva, located in Mount Zion after 1967, says that the Vatican will turn it into a pilgrimage site for hundreds of thousands of Catholics and hold religious services there.

In fact, during his visit to Israel in 2000, Pope John Paul II held mass in the Hall of Last Supper. The Pope knew that the site had a strategic location, as it is just a few hundred yards from the Temple Mount and adjacent to the Old City walls. Israel should not be bowing to the Vatican, as the Jewish State is admirably committed to protecting the holy sites of all religions and guaranteeing the right of worship for all faiths. However, instead of saying "keep your hands off Jerusalem, It is not for sale," the Israeli government accepted the Vatican's ransom. In the long term, the gesture will increase tensions between Jews and the tremendously large assets of the Vatican. The Holy See has long been working to reduce Jewish rights in Jerusalem and in the Old City. Now, after the Muslim Waqf authority expelled the Christians from the site and turned it into a mosque, it is the turn of the Vatican to lay its hands on Jewish Jerusalem.

Instead of cooperating with the Jewish state and recognizing that the only way to guarantee religious freedom is by maintaining the unity of Jerusalem under Israeli sovereignty, the Vatican embraces the cause of ending Jewish sovereignty.

Hillel Weiss, the Bar-Ilan University professor for literature and one of the bravest public voices in Israel, published an article titled "The pope – a persona non grata."[89] Professor Weiss criticized Benedict's visit to the Temple Mount. "The goal is that a Jew's foot will not step on the heart of Jerusalem, like before the year 5727 (1967), and in fact just like today and since the liberation of Jerusalem," wrote Weiss. A document released for the Pope's visit by the Jewish Sanhedrin, of which Professor Weiss is a senior member, reads, "For many years negotiations and contacts to reach agreements have been conducted regarding what the Catholic Church sees as its property or desires for itself, whether within previous confines such as Mt. Zion or within the Old City, the Kinneret, and other places. Those who initiated the concept of the 'Holy Basin' principally intend to remove exclusive Jewish sovereignty from the Temple Mount and the Old City and in effect, aim at the total removal of Jewish sovereignty."[90] It means a return to a time when half of Israel's capital was under Arab control, the Old City was closed to Jews, the synagogues were systematically desecrated, and walls, barbed wire, and snipers divided the city by force.

When the Vatican calls for the "internationalization" and "extraterritoriality" of Jerusalem, it isn't interested in "access to the Holy Sites," which the Church already has under Israeli law for their institutions and assets in Jerusalem. Also, when these "Holy Sites" were under the jurisdiction of the Jordanians from 1948-1967, no Pope demanded the "internationalization of Jerusalem."[91] It is something else that the Vatican wants. What the Vatican wants is the end of Jewish control of Jerusalem. In all its usages, "Judaization" has been an accusation against Jews, not just Israelis, when the majority of them were living in Europe. In the 16th century, in Poland many towns obtained the so called "privilegia de non tolerandis Judaeis," cities in which the Jews were forbidden to

---

89 Ynetnews, April 5, 2009
90 http://www.thesanhedrin.org/en/index.php?title=Psak_5769_Nisan_1
91 "Les lieux saints" by B. Collin, Paris, 1968

live. Europe had Jewish ghettos during the Middle Ages and zoning restrictions in Czarist Russia.

The Catholic Church wants Israel to relinquish sovereignty at the Western Wall and the Temple Mount. This is the "Holy Basin" formula, which refers to the area of the "Noble Sanctuary," the Mount of Olives, Mount Zion and a variety of Christian holy sites. In 1964, when Pope Paul VI made the first papal visit to Jerusalem, the city was divided by barbed-wire and snipers crouched on the roofs. Jews and Christians with Israeli passports were barred from entering the Old City, in violation of Article 8 of the 1949 Armistice Agreement. At that time, the Vatican ambassador's residence at the foot of the Mount of Olives, provided a close look at the razing of over 40,000 Jewish graves in Judaism's oldest cemetery and where, according to tradition, the resurrection of the dead on the Day of Judgment will happen. The Vatican never raised its voice to protest against the apartheid imposed by the Jordanians. Israeli leaders asked the Vatican to use its "good offices" to intervene in order to stop the desecration, but during this dark period, the rape of Jewish Jerusalem did not lead to any expression of concern from Vatican diplomats.

The Catholic Church, which has discovered "rights" in Jerusalem, stood totally silent from 1948 to 1967, when its representatives witnessed systematic pillaging of the Jewish synagogues and systematic racism against Jewish pilgrims. Since Israel reunited the city, followers of all three monotheistic faiths have been able to worship without restrictions, with the only apartheid that existed imposed on Jews on Judaism's holiest site, the Temple Mount, which though under Israeli sovereignty, is controlled by the Muslim Wakf. No Israeli government must tolerate any policy of division, "shared control" or "internationalization" that opens the door to a return to the Arab apartheid between 1948 and 1967. The Vatican never raised a cry for internationalization during that time. Instead of making blatantly political agreements with the Arabs, Catholic leaders should cooperate with the Jews and recognize that the only way to guarantee religious freedom is by maintaining the unity of

Jerusalem under Israeli sovereignty. And to recognize the unique role and place of the Jews and Israel in the world.

The Catholic denial of Israel's claim to the land goes beyond the Temple Mount. The Palestinian Authority has been able to list Bethlehem's Church of the Nativity as its first world heritage site under the United Nations' cultural agency, UNESCO. The PLO knows the consequences of locating King David's and Jesus' city as being in the "country of Palestine." The final goal is the de-Judaization of the land of Israel. Oras Hamdan Taha, the Palestinian minister who deals with antiquities and gets funds from UNESCO, made clear, this goal is "writing or rewriting the history of Palestine."[92]

Next in line is Rachel's Tomb, Judaism's third most holy site, or as the Jews say in Hebrew, "Rahel Imenu," and in Yiddish, "Mame Rochel" — our Mother Rachel. In the book of Genesis, the Bible says, "And Rachel died, and was buried on the way to Ephrata, which is Bethlehem. And Jacob set a pillar upon her grave: That is the pillar of Rachel's grave unto this day." For millennia, Rachel's Tomb, alongside the road between Jerusalem and Bethlehem, has served as a place of longing, pilgrimage, and prayer for the Jewish people, although there is some controversy about the grave's exact location. Only in 1996, the Palestinians began referring to the site as the "Bilal ibn Rabah Mosque," as UNESCO shamefully listed it in 2010.[93] The PLO enrolled the tomb as a weapon in the Second Intifada, claiming the site and shooting at the Jewish worshippers on a daily basis. On Yom Kippur 2000, six days after the Israeli army retreated from Joseph's Tomb in Nablus, the PLO newspaper Al-Hayat al-Jadida published an article explaining that Rachel's Tomb was the next Palestinian target. Before the PLO's propaganda, the Arabs simply referred to the site as "Kubat Rahil," the dome of Rachel. What is unknown is that the Christian institutions in Judea and Samaria are collaborating with the

---

92 "Rewriting history? P.A. claims ancient Shechem," CBN News, August 14 2011
93 The Jerusalem Post, November 8, 2010

Muslims to destroy and deny the Jewish character of the sacred site. And the strategy has already proven to be very successful.

In February of 2012, UNESCO, which has accepted the Palestinian Authority as a state, claimed that Rachel's Tomb and the Tomb of the Patriarchs are not exclusively Jewish sites, but "also belong to Christians and Muslims." The Christian Fadi Kattan denied "the Jewishness" and "the exclusiveness of Jewish access to Rachel's Tomb".[94]

It was in a meeting with Christian leaders that, in March 2010, Chief Islamic Judge, Tayseer Tamimi, called on Muslim and Christian leaders to take immediate action against Israel's attempts to "Judaize" Jerusalem and "the Bilal ibn Rabah Mosque." Pax Christi, one of the most famous global Catholic organizations, in its website, repeatedly calls the Jewish site a "mosque." Then there is the Bethlehem University of the Holy Land, the only Vatican-run educational institution in the area and whose founding can be traced back to the visit of Pope Paul VI in the holy land in 1964. The Catholic University recently launched a project about Rachel's Tomb. The document calls it "a historical religious site for followers of Christianity and Islam, a sacred site also for Jews, who today control all access to it, despite its location on Palestinian lands." The Vatican institution seems to ignore that Rachel's Tomb belongs to Area C, which the Oslo Accords gave to Israeli jurisdiction.

The very title of the Catholic project, "Rachel: An Alien in her Hometown," suggests that the tomb is a spot hijacked by the Israelis. The tomb, the Catholic report says, "is also known by Muslims as the Bilal Ibn Rabah Mosque." According to the Vatican university, the Jews stole the past, the Jewish shrines are Arab treasures stolen by the Zionists, and the Jews are no more than invading colonizers.

Two years ago when I last visited Rachel's Tomb, the Israeli contractor who worked at the security barrier showed me the Arab

---

[94] "Bethlehemites Are Palestinian Christians," Palestine Chronicle, June 26, 2011

houses from where the Palestinian snipers shot at the Jews visiting the grave. Down below, there is the romantic, medieval picture of the once modest, quiet, calm, serene and solitary domed tomb. The 20th century of Joseph Goebbels has taught all of us that a lie starts as a small one, but if it is not corrected, it festers like a "cancer" destroying truth, justice and finally — people. A lesson that the Catholics should have learned much better. Now Rachel's Tomb is like a bunker, highly protected by walls, barbed wire, soldiers, cameras, corridors. But who will protect it from horrible lies?

Giulio Meotti

3. ZIONISM IS RACISM

In 1986 John Pawlikowski of the Catholic Theological Union of Chicago urged that Jewish-Christian dialogue give special attention to Zionism. He declared that "no Christian-Jewish dialogue can be complete" without the movement that led to re-establishing the Jewish state of Israel.[95] Pawlikowski said if Christians continue to exclude Zionism from the discussion, "they are in fact asking for a dialogue with an emaciated form of Judaism."[96]

Unfortunately, a century of visceral anti-Zionism had planted deep roots in the Catholic conscience.[97] During the 20th century, the Vatican represented the de-Judaization of Palestine and the hatred for Zionists as pious deeds. The anti-Zionist stance was supported by an international network of Catholic hierarchies, lay Catholic organizations and the Catholic press. Leading this international Catholic lobby against Zionism were the Catholic bishops of the United States.[98] In Arab Christian circles, Islam became the savior of Christianity against the Jews. Christian proponents of Arabism were recruited among clergy, civil servants, intellectuals and diplomats linked to the Vatican, and the Catholic French diplomacy. Serving Islamic aims, Syrian and Palestinian Christians propagated Arab theses of Jewish evilness. Christian ideologists, such as the proto-Nazi Antun Sa'adé, or the cofounder

---

[95] "Catholic theologian says no to exclusion of Zionism," Boca Raton News, October 25, 1986
[96] The New York Times, December 18, 1987
[97] For the early Church's opposition to the creation of a Jewish State, see "The Vatican and Zionism. Conflict in the Holy Land, 1895-1925," by Sergio Minerbi, Oxford University Press (1990)
[98] "The Vatican, American Catholics and the Struggle for Palestine, 1917-1958," by Adriano Ercole Ciani, School of Graduate and Postdoctoral Studies University of Western Ontario London, Ontario, Canada

of the Baath party, Michel Aflaq, advocated the theology of "Palestinianism."

The first Arabic translation of "The Protocols of Elders of Zion," the most infamous and lethal anti-Jewish forgery, appeared in the *Raqib Shayun* (15 January 1926), published by the Catholic Church in Jerusalem.[99] After the Balfour Declaration of 1917, Vatican opposition to Jewish territorial sovereignty in the Holy Land grew more entrenched. In the years after the Holocaust, Vatican anti-Zionist policies attempted to block the partition of Palestine at the United Nations, and to secure Jerusalem as an international, sovereign "corpus separatum."[100]

Two major cardinals were active in British Palestine in the first twenty years of the 20th century: the British Francis Bourne and the Italian Filippo Giustini. Cardinal Bourne in January 1919 sent a letter to then British government and to the Foreign secretary, writing that Zionism had not received the approval of the Vatican, and if the Jews would "ever again dominate and rule the country, it would be an outrage to Christianity and its Divine founder."[101] Cardinal Giustini in October 1919 cabled the Pope from Jerusalem asking for his intervention "to prevent the re-establishment of Zionist Israel in Palestine." In 1919 another Pope, Benedict XIV, called the Jews "infidels" whose coming to power would cause "terrible grief for us." In a letter from Jerusalem, dated 25 January 1919, Cardinal Francis Bourne, Catholic Archbishop of Westminster, defined Zionism as "contrary to Christian sensitivity and tradition."[102]

The period between the first Zionist conference in 1897 and the creation of the State of Israel was marked by many episodes of anti-Semitism by the Vatican. In 1897, the Jesuit magazine Civiltà Cattolica, a semi official Holy See newspaper, published an

[99] "Islam and Dhimmitude" by Bat Ye'or, Farleigh (2001)
[100] "The Catholic Church and the Question of Palestine" by Livia Rokach, Saqi Books, 1987
[101] "Occasional sermons" by Bourne F., Sheed and Ward, 1930
[102] "The Roman Catholic Question in the Anglo-Jewish Press, 1890-1925" by Simon Mayers, Melilah, January 2010

editorial in which it claimed that "the Jewish people have to remain dispersed," and that "a resurrected Israelite kingdom is contrary to the Christ's predictions."[103] Shortly after the 1897 Basle Conference which promoted the Zionist return of the Jews to their homeland, Civiltà Cattolica gave its biblical-theological judgment on political Zionism: "1827 years have passed since the prediction of Jesus of Nazareth was fulfilled... that after the destruction of Jerusalem the Jews would be led away to be slaves among all the nations and that they would remain in the dispersion until the end of the world." The Jews should not be permitted to return to Palestine with sovereignty: "According to the Sacred Scriptures, the Jewish people must always live dispersed and *vagabondo* (wandering) among the other nations, so that they may render witness to Christ not only by the Scriptures... but by their very existence."

Civiltà Cattolica has been the faithful interpreter of papal thought and gained an influence far beyond Catholic circles. Until 1933, its contributors remained anonymous. In 1922 the Civiltà Cattolica complained that the Zionists returning to Palestine had "forgotten that more that 1,800 years had passed since their faith, smitten by the divine malediction, or if this sounds unpleasant, subjugated by a hand stronger than theirs, were expelled and dispersed over the whole earth." So applies that Christian anti-Semitic tradition of divine punishment of the Jews, for the killing and rejection of Jesus. The Jews have forsaken all rights to God's promises, and thus to Eretz Yisrael, the biblical land of Israel. They should continue to wander the earth, as did Cain. Civiltà wrote of "Jewish hatred... against mankind," of the "anti-social spirit of Judaism," and of the "necessity of hating it."

Worst of all was the review's attitude concerning the blood libel. Civiltà Cattolica wrote of the Jews of Trent, "mingling unleavened bread with Christian blood, every year, at Passover," and of the "present Jewish use of Christian blood in paschal bread and wine."

---

[103] "La segregazione amichevole. 'La Civiltà Cattolica' e la questione ebraica" by Barbara Raggi e Ruggero Taradel, Edizioni Riuniti, 2000

Civiltà dwelt further on "the reality of the use of Christian blood in many rituals of the modern synagogue." Three years after the advent of the Third Reich, Civiltà competed with Nazi propaganda, stating that the Jews "have become the masters of the world"; "Their prototype is the banker, and their supreme ideal to turn the world into an incorporated joint-stock company."

In search of a solution to the "Jewish Question" Civiltà analyzed Zionism. Would the Jews, asked the writer, once they had realized the Zionist state, "give up their messianic aspiration to world domination and preponderance, both capitalistic and revolutionary? Besides, what would be the attitude of the Christians when they saw the Holy Places in Jewish hands?" As Civiltà Cattolica saw it, the only way to salvation was through conversion. The magazine declared that "the Zionism is invading the Arab house," "Zionism is anti-Christian and anti-Catholic." Throughout World War II, Civiltà's silence over the fate of the Jews echoed that of Pius XII. Civiltà Cattolica wrote on 19 June, 1948: "Two Zionist emissaries were arrested in Gaza and were accused of having poisoned the wells of the city. According to documented evidence, they had also spread typhoid and dysentery germs in many water sources."[104]

Another example was the article entitled "The dangerous influence of Zionism" by G. de Vries published in Civiltà Cattolica in April 1950 that described the newly established State of Israel as "racist" and "fanatic" and "infected by the worst kind of materialism... substantially due to Soviet influence." Despite this scornful judgment in Rome, Theodore Herzl hoped for papal support for the Zionist dream. In late January 1904, after the sixth Zionist Congress and six months before his death, Herzl travelled to Rome, and crossed the Tiber to the Vatican. Herzl first met the Secretary of State, Cardinal Merry del Val. According to Herzl's diary, the Cardinal replied that "the history of Israel is our own history, it is our foundation. But in order that we should come out

---

[104] "Poison. Manifestations of a blood libel" by Raphael Israeli, Lexington 2002

for the Jewish people in the way that you desire, they should first have to accept conversion."

Three days later Herzl met Pope Pius X. Again from Herzl's diary: the Pope replied to Herzl's outline of the Jewish Return: "We are unable to favor this movement. We cannot prevent the Jews going to Jerusalem, but we could never sanction it... The Jews have not recognized our Lord, therefore we cannot recognize the Jewish people." That was in 1904. Most likely the Zionist movement would have fallen apart but for a succession of events which neither Herzl nor anyone else could foresee: World War I, the collapse of the Ottoman empire, the British conquest of Palestine and its being placed by the League of Nations under the UK Mandate (1922), and the 1924 immigration quotas by the American government. The British would try to be loyal to the pledge of the 1917 Balfour Declaration: "the establishment in Palestine of a national home for the Jewish people."

In the Vatican, Pius X's theological underpinnings for the opposition to Zionism were still intact and vehement. Fearful of the declaration and Britain's conquest of Palestine in 1917, the Secretary of State, Pietro Cardinal Gasparri, remarked: "It is hard to take back that part of our heart which has been given over to the Turks in order to give it to the Zionists."[105] On 6 March 1922, Gasparri severely criticized the draft British Mandate for Palestine as being incompatible with the Covenant of the League of Nations. The British plan would establish "an absolute economic, administrative and political preponderance of Jews."[106]

In January 1919 the Franciscans of Jerusalem, who had the Vatican task of taking care of the holy sites, published a violent document against Zionism. Cardinal Pietro Gasparri (1852-1934), who was Secretary of State under two Popes (Benedict XV and his successor Pius XI) said that "the most dangerous threat is the creation of a Jewish State in Palestine." Gasparri claimed that, "It is better the internationalization of the Holy Sites rather than to

---

105 See "The Vatican and Zionism" by Minerbi
106 "Zionism and the State of Israel" by Michael Prior, Routledge, 1999

see Jerusalem in the hands of the Jews." Pope Pius X in a message to cardinal Giustini hoped that "a Zionist regime, already despised by Him, won't wound the Christian conscience." In that period many anti-Semitic articles by the French writer R. Lambelin were published by L'Osservatore Romano. Lambelin later translated into French the proto-Nazi libel "Protocols of the Elders of Zion."

In 1922, while discussions were underway at the League of Nations on the subject of the British mandate for Palestine, the future president of Israel Chaim Weizmann made a very interesting observation: "The Catholics have been chiefly responsible for uniting the Muslims and the Christians against us, because what the Vatican really wishes to have is something which amounts to power in Palestine, and it has been using various Catholic members of the League, such as Spain, Brazil, Italy, Belgium and France, in order to achieve its object, and this is really the inner meaning of its attacks against us."

Then Latin patriarch of Jerusalem, Luigi Barlassina, condemned the creation of an "autocratic Zionist domination."[107] L'Osservatore Romano published dozens of Barlassina's articles against the Jews "displacing the original inhabitants of the Palestine to create a Zionist kingdom." Barlassina also said that the Zionist movement "declared war to all Catholics and Arabs" and spreads "immorality, anarchy and communism." According to Barlassina, "the very stones are crying out for vengeance. The Catholic world must fight against the profanation of the Holy Land by the Zionists. It must declare a holy war against Zionism." Bishop Umberto Benigni in 1921 said that the Vatican had to fight against the "Israel of the Talmud."

On May 1921 the Jewish workers in Jaffa organized a parade on the streets. The Arabs attacked it and 50 Jews and the same number of Arabs were killed and many hundreds wounded. Instead of condemning the Arab attackers, a few days later the

---

[107] See Sergio Minerbi

L'Osservatore Romano explained that "the Bolsheviks" had infiltrated into Palestine thanks to the Zionist Organization. The paper also raised the question whether the Communist revolution was coordinated with Zionism or whether Zionism raised a red atheistic viper in its bosom.

A few days later, Pope Benedict XV attacked Zionism in his allocution to the cardinals of 13 June 1921. He said that the Jews were given a "position of preponderance and privilege in Palestine"; that their activity is meant "to take away the sacred character of the Holy Places."[108] He admitted that no damage should "be done to the rights of the Jewish element," but "they must in no way be put above the just rights of the Christians."

As Sergio Minerbi explained in his magisterial book on the Vatican and Zionism in the first half of the century, in the Twenties the Catholic Church "believed the Zionists were antireligious people, that Zionist immigration would sweep the Christians out of Palestine and destroy the Christian character of the country, and that the Jews were causing radical changes in the traditional life-style of the local population damaging moral values. During that period the Vatican was strongly opposed to Jewish statehood in the Holy Land." In August 1929 the Arabs attacked the Jewish quarters in Hebron, in Safed and other places, killing dozens of Jews in a pogrom reminiscent to that of Kishinev. The L'Osservatore Romano, rather than blaming the Arabs for the attack, wrote that it was "the politics of Zionism, and not the religion of Israel, which lay at the root of the trouble."

In the same line of thought, Domenico Tardini, the Vatican Undersecretary of State, told a British diplomat in 1938: "There was no real reason why the Jews should be back in Palestine. Why should not a nice place be found for them, for instance in South America?"[109] The Vatican opposed the Balfour declaration at the League of Nations, it endorsed the anti-British "White Paper," which fought the Jews' right to immigrate to their holy land.

---

108 "Israel and the holy places of Christendom" by Zandel W., Weidenfeld 1972
109 "The rise of Israel" by Jonathan Adelman, Routledge

Archbishop Angelo Roncalli, later to become Pope John XXIII and recognized by some Jews as a friend, wrote that he was "uneasy about the attempts of Jews to reach Palestine, as if they were trying to reconstruct a Jewish kingdom."[110] That was while the Shoah was already raging and hundreds of thousands of Jews were being killed by the Nazis. Even then, anti-Zionist attitudes prevailed among the Vatican diplomats.

Cardinal Maglione, Secretary of State, wrote in May 1943 to his Apostolic Delegate in the United States, Cicognani, that it would not be difficult "if one wants to establish a 'Jewish Home,' to find other territories (territories other than Palestine) which could better fulfill this aim, while Palestine, under Jewish predominance, would bring new and grave international problems." Josef Stalin had the same idea in the Soviet Union's Birobidzan. Cardinal Maglione wrote in the same month that "Catholics would be wounded in their religious sentiment and would rightly fear for their rights if Palestine became the exclusive property of the Jews." In August 1944 the Secretariat of State of the Holy See wrote that they regarded Palestine "not as a Jewish home or a possible Arab Home but also as a Catholic Home and Catholic Centre."

When in Auschwitz and Treblinka, Jews were being gassed with Zyklon B, Vatican's Undersecretary of State Domenico Tardini (under Pope Pius XII) opposed Jewish emigration to Palestine, the only place where Jews could have been saved: "The Holy See has never approved of the project of making Palestine a Jewish home... because Palestine is by now holier for Catholics than for Jews." In the fall of 1944, a memorandum prepared by the Vatican's Secretariat of State for Pius XII before his meeting with Winston Churchill, stated that "the Holy See has always been opposed to Jewish domination in Palestine." At the peak of the Holocaust, the Vatican's main thought was to oppose the creation of a Jewish State. Pope Pius XII made known to President Franklin D. Roosevelt his opposition toward a Jewish homeland. Dated June

---

[110] Time for candor from the Church," Jerusalem Post, February 11, 1991

22, 1943, the letter sent by Amleto Cicognani, the Pope's special representative to the US, to Ambassador Myron Taylor, Roosevelt's emissary to Pius XII, made clear Pius's policy against Zionism.[111] "It is true that at one time Palestine was inhabited by the Hebrew Race, but there is no axiom in history to substantiate the necessity of a people returning to a country they left nineteen centuries before," the letter reads. "If a 'Hebrew Home' is desired, it would not be too difficult to find a more fitting territory than Palestine. With an increase in the Jewish population there, grave, new international problems would arise."[112]

On 10 April 1945, while the war was still going on in Europe, Moshè Sharet of the Jewish Agency, was received by Pope Pius XII. He hoped for the "moral support" of the Catholic Church for "our renewed existence in Palestine." But he did not receive any support; on the contrary the Holy See started a new campaign for "the internationalization of Jerusalem" supported by France, another name used to deprive the Jews of their homeland. The Vatican considered Zionism to be "an enemy," only suitable to be the basis for a new alliance between Christians and Moslems in Palestine. Catholic bishops in the United States then urged US President, Harry Truman, not to admit Israel to the United Nations.

L'Osservatore Romano, the official Vatican daily, "welcomed" the proclamation of the State of Israel on May 14, 1948 by these words: "Modern Israel is not the true heir of Biblical Israel, but a secular state... The Holy Land and its sacred sites belong to Christianity, the True Israel."[113] In July 1949, La Documentation Catholique, the official bulletin of the French Catholic Church, declared: "We can only agree with a statement frequently heard that Zionism is Nazism in a new guise." The Vatican called the creation of Israel "another tragic milestone in the Via Crucis of

[111] "Accuse da Israele: 'Pio XII si oppose allo stato ebraico'," Il Corriere della Sera, July 4, 1999
[112] "The Arab lobby" by Mitchel Bard, Broadside Books, 2010
[113] "Vatican Policy on the Palestinian-Israeli Conflict" by Andrej Kreutz, Greenwood Press

Palestine."[114] In 1947 Great Britain decided to renounce the Mandate and to deliver the Palestine issue over to the United Nations. The General Assembly approved, on November 29, 1947, resolution 181 on the partition of Palestine and the creation of a "corpus separatum" for Jerusalem and its surroundings.

After the war L'Osservatore Romano wrote that "the sacrifice of Christ" was a "prohibition of any claim to the promised land." Giorgio Hakim, then Catholic bishop of San Giovanni d'Acri, in 1947 delivered to the Pope in the Vatican a letter by the Muftì of Jerusalem — who had been an ally to Hitler in the "final solution" — against Israel's project. Pius XII reacted "very cordially".[115] When Israel was fighting four Arab armies which wanted to annihilate the Jewish State, the American Catholic press gave wide circulation to the public appeal of British Archbishop Arthur Hughes, the apostolic nuncio to Egypt, who charged the "deliberate Jewish efforts to decimate the Arabs and destroy Christianity in Palestine," and the "particular hatred" that Jews had demonstrated against Catholic institutions. By the summer of 1948, the Catholic press and the Vatican officials attempted to tie the Arab Christian refugee crisis into its general critique of "Israeli incursions," and "Jewish imperialism." Fantastic slander typical of the worst anti-Israel propaganda.[116]

The most important Catholic intellectuals of the time used the pre-war anti-Semitic propaganda against the Jewish State. "Is it true that in Tel Aviv there are no synagogues?" asked the French writer Francois Mauriac in the paper Le Figaro. And Louis Massignon condemned the "spiritual betrayal of Zionism." In 1949 the Italian embassy in the Vatican dispatched a message that the Holy See had the opinion that "the Israelis are using against the Arabs the same methods that the Nazis used against them."

The Vatican hatred for Jewish sovereignty would have a deep echo in the decades following the war. In 1997 Moshe Sasson, a

---

[114] See Minerbi
[115] "Vaticano e Israele" by Silvio Ferrari, Sansoni, 1991
[116] "Aria di crociata" by Paolo Zanini, Edizioni Unicopli, 2012

former Israeli ambassador in Rome, revealed to the daily newspaper Maariv that in 1976 Israeli officials had asked the Vatican to withdraw the Holy See's support for the UN resolution that compared "Zionism to Racism." Sasson told Agostino Casaroli, Vatican foreign minister at the time, that Israel would consider the Catholic's support of that resolution as a "spiritual war by the Catholic Church against Judaism."[117]

On November 10, 1975, Daniel Patrick Moynihan, America's ambassador to the UN proclaimed, "The United States... does not acknowledge, it will not abide by, it will never acquiesce in this infamous act." The "infamous act" was Resolution 3379, calling Zionism racism, and slandering Jewish independence. That same day, Israel's ambassador Chaim Herzog, carrying the dignity of 4,000 years of Jewish history, declared, "I stand here not as a supplicant... for the issue is neither Israel nor Zionism. The issue is the continued existence of this organization, which has been dragged to its lowest point of discredit by a coalition of despots and racists... You yourselves bear the responsibility for your stand before history... We, the Jewish people, will not forget."[118] The resolution set a template for attacking Israel and Zionism using human rights rhetoric. That resolution became one of Israel's most dramatic political-diplomatic struggles. Defense minister Moshe Dayan said UN resolutions were not worth the paper on which they were written, while foreign minister Yigal Allon declared: "Zionism can take care of itself — it is the UN which is in mortal danger."

Nobody remembered that two years before that infamous resolution, when Israel was risking a new Holocaust under the military threat of the Arab nations, a statement which the seven Catholic and Orthodox churches in Iraq transmitted to Rome said, "Zionism is a racialist movement hostile to all accepted human values and linked to world imperialism. It is far removed from Judaism as a religion." A Muslim-Catholic major Conference also

[117] Ansa News Agency, August 21, 1997
[118] http://domino.un.org/pdfs/APV2400.pdf

took place in Tripoli, Libya.[119] It was a collection of theologians, historians, politicians, scholars and bishops. The conference was held under the patronage of Colonel Muammar Gaddafi, the Chairman of Libya's Revolutionary Command Council, but also then, one of the major terrorist patrons. Christians were represented by the Vatican. Some Orthodox and Protestant Churches sent observers. Islam was represented by scholars from Libya, Sudan, Syria, Palestine, Pakistan, Algeria, Tunisia, and Lebanon. These Islamic countries were all deniers of Israel's right to exist. The Vatican delegation, precise, practiced, its papers well prepared, was supported by a battalion of priests, monks, bishops and Catholic theologians. The atmosphere was described as "remarkably harmonious." The Libyans were welcoming and caring. The conference began on a cool Sunday afternoon.

Cardinal Sergio Pignedoli,[120] leader of the Vatican Delegation, benign, smiling, asserted the "two essential values" shared by religions: the love of God and the brotherhood of man. At the final session of the conference twenty-four declarations were presented. The document was very similar to the UN resolution against the right to life of the Jewish people. Four of the twelve members of the Vatican delegation and four of the twelve Muslims were given the task of preparing the statement. "The name of Tripoli will live in history," said Father Rossano as he concluded his job of rapporteur. The two sides affirmed their belief in God, "the Only One" honoring "all Prophets and apostles in all revealed Religions."

The Vatican and Islamic sides claimed that "religion is the basis of true legislation and that all legislations enacted by man alone will never reach the acme of perfection."[121] Then they came to the most tragic chapter: "The Two Parties look upon revealed religion with respect, and accordingly they distinguish between Judaism and Zionism, the latter being a racial aggressive movement, foreign

[119] "The Link," Volume 9, Number 1, 1976
[120] New York Times, June 16, 1980
[121] Catholic Herald, February 13, 1976

to Palestine and the entire Eastern region." After this inter-religious fatwa against Israel and the Jews, the Vatican signed also this part of the final document: "Abiding by Truth and Justice and being fully concerned with Peace and believing in the right of people for self-determination, the Two Parties reaffirm the national rights of the Palestinian people and their right to return to their homeland, and to affirm the Arabism of the city of Jerusalem, and the rejection of Judaization, partition and internationalization projects and denounce any violation of all sacred shrines. The Two Sides request the setting free of all the detainees in occupied Palestine, above all the Muslim 'Ulema and the Christian clergy; they also demand the liberation of all occupied territories and call for the formation of a permanent commission to investigate the alteration of sacred Muslim and Christian sites and reveal all these to the world's public opinion."

Bishop Ignatius, Patriarch of Lebanon, also declared: "I consider world Zionism the greatest challenge to Christianity and Islam in this world." The gravity of the Vatican participation in this conference is also due to the fact that Cardinal Pignedoli was one of the leading contenders for the papacy. A close friend and adviser of Pope Paul VI, Cardinal Pignedoli was reported to be Paul's choice as his successor. He was again counted as a "papabile" — a possible pope — when Paul's successor, John Paul I, died in September 1978 after 34 days on the papal throne. In 1976 the Vatican voted in favor of the Declaration of Principles of the UN Habitat Conference in Vancouver, which condemned Zionism as Racism.[122] The resolution, rejected by 15 Western countries because anti-Israel, "contained a reference to 'all forms of racial discrimination' mentioned in resolutions adopted by the United Nations General Assembly. This obviously included the Assembly's resolution of the previous November, defining Zionism as a form of racism."[123]

---

[122] "Vatican Vote on Zionism," Catholic Herald, June 18, 1976
[123] "Vatican Supports 'habitat' Declaration Considered Anti-israel," Jewish Telegraphic Agency, June 18, 1976

Victor Lucas, President of the Anglo-Jewish Association, writing in the Catholic Herald newspaper declared, "We are concerned because this declaration repeats the notorious 'Zionism is Racism' libel, and surprised because most European countries including Britain, Italy and France had voted against it. I am anxious lest Catholic/Jewish relations should be damaged, particularly at a time when a warm understanding between our two communities was steadily growing following Vatican II. Please convey our deep disquiet to the Holy See." This history of Vatican anti-Zionism explains why Israel's founder and first prime minister, David Ben-Gurion, said that "for the Vatican the power of Israel is a theological threat."

4. BLESSING THE INTIFADA

Arafat in Rome and Jesus the Palestinian

It was Pope John Paul II's privilege to give a papal audience to anyone he wished. But he and the Vatican officials made a tragic choice by granting several audiences to Yasser Arafat, head of the Palestine Liberation Organization, the terrorist seeking to win for the Arabs not only the territories liberated by Israel in 1967, but 1948-Israel itself. Arafat and his followers had shed the blood of Jewish schoolchildren and athletes, politicians and passers-by, in and beyond the Middle East. His organization's actions had horrified the world. By meeting the Pope, Arafat was not seeking guidance; he was seeking publicity and legitimacy at a time the PLO Covenant declared that "the establishment of Israel is fundamentally null and void,"[124] and that "the claim of historical or spiritual ties between the Jews and Palestine does not tally with historical realities." The Pope gave him what he was looking for.

Future generations will wonder how a murderous organization such as the PLO had been able, in spite of its proudly proclaimed barbarism and anti-Semitism, to achieve world-wide acclaim, respectability and support from the Catholic Church. The Nazi charter written in 1920 can be compared to the Palestinian manifesto of Cairo, 1968. Out of the 33 articles in the Arab covenant, 30 of them directly or indirectly call for the use of violence against the Jews. The document encompasses moral, utilitarian, volitional, legal and military arguments, all of which converge into a negation, as a matter of principle, of the existence

---

[124] http://www.jewishvirtuallibrary.org/jsource/Terrorism/PLO_Covenant.html

of the State of Israel in any form or size, from Nazareth to Beersheba through Shechem.

The Palestinian covenant rejects the idea that Jews have any "historical or religious ties" to the land, since "Judaism, being a religion, is not an independent nationality." Here the influence of Vatican Council is clear. The covenant proclaims violence against unarmed Israeli civilians, as in Article 9: "Armed struggle is the only way to liberate Palestine." It is not a manifesto of an extreme, lunatic group, but the essence and mainstream of the Palestinian story. If the PLO charter says that Palestine is an "indivisible" part of the Arab world and the Palestinians of the Arab nation, the Nazi manifesto demands the union of all Germans in Europe to form a Great Germany. Palestine itself is defined in Article 2 as going well beyond the West Bank and Gaza Strip, to encompass the whole of Israel proper. If the Palestinians consider the Balfour Declaration null and void, the Nazis demanded the abolition of the Versailles peace treaty. If the PLO covenant is defined as "not to be amended" (in fact it was never reformed), the Nazi chart is declared to be unalterable.

PLO's article six declares: "The Jews who had normally resided in Palestine until the beginning of the Zionist invasion (usually dated as the mid-19th century) will be considered Palestinians." In other words, about 95 per cent of the existing Israeli Jewish population is to be banished or killed. Why did the Vatican give legitimacy to this proto-Nazi ethnic cleansing? Like Hitlerism, Palestinianism is not a national identity, but a criminal ideological construct developed as part of a terrorist agenda when the PLO was created in 1964. Now the question is whether the creation of a PLO state in Judea and Samaria is the key to Arab-Jew peace. One danger of such a state is that it would establish a full-fledged army which would be stationed along border areas adjacent to the cities containing 70 percent of Israel's population. Would the PLO now sue for peace if the territories were returned? The question was answered with blunt candor by Zahariya Abdel Rahin, a former PLO political director who said, "The fundamental Palestinian issue is not just the lands that were occupied in 1967 but every inch of Palestine."

The PLO manifesto claims that the "Palestinian personality" is an "innate, persistent characteristic that does not disappear... and is transferred from fathers to sons" (No. 4). Could Heinrich Himmler have said it better? Like the Nazis who tried to conquer their "Lebensraum" in Europe, the PLO never gave up the nightmare of creating an Arab Lebensraum. In 1981, the late Jewish philosopher Emil Fackenheim wrote in the Globe and Mail: "The covenant can be amended only by a two-thirds majority (No. 33). No attempt has ever been made to amend it. In assassinating dissidents within its own ranks, the PLO does no more than abide by the document to which it is committed. If this is what it does to its own people, one can imagine what it would do to Israelis, if it were ever given the opportunity by weakness on the part of Israel or folly on the part of the world."

That is why Israel's Prime Minister, Menachem Begin, railed against the Pope's decision to meet the terrorist leader. Begin said that Pope's hands had been "stained with the blood of innocent Jewish children." Another unnamed Israeli official, who some believed to be Begin again, expressed his outrage in these words: "The Church, which did not say a word about the massacre of the Jews for six years in Europe and has not had much to say about the killing of Christians for seven years in Lebanon, is now ready to meet a man who committed the killings in Lebanon and who wants the destruction of Israel in order to complete the work carried out by the Nazis in Germany... If this man (Pope John Paul II) meets with Arafat, it is indicative of a certain moral standard."

John Paul II sullied his papacy with a nauseating, twenty-minute meeting with Yasser Arafat on September 16, 1982 — long before the PLO chief feigned his formal renunciation of terrorism. The pontiff went on to meet Arafat ten more times. The Vatican gave Arafat a platform of immense resonance throughout the international community.

In 1989 the meeting of Cardinal Cassaroli, Secretary of State for the Vatican, with Farouk Kadumi, director of the Political Department of the Palestine Liberation Organization, also raised serious questions. Emerging from the meeting, Kadumi announced that "there is no doubt that the Vatican's position is that of solidarity with the Palestinian people in its liberation struggle."[125] Kadumi also stated that "as regards the Middle East crisis, the role of the Holy See, and especially of the Pope, might be very significant considering its moral, religious and, therefore, political weight with the states and peoples in the area." PLO leadership has not wavered from its intention of destroying the State of Israel, nor has it ever indicated a willingness to recognize Israel or negotiate peacefully with its democratically elected representatives. Indeed, Kadumi is on record as having affirmed PLO deadly intentions with the statement that "the Zionist ghetto of Israel must be destroyed."[126]

The reaction in Israel to Cardinal Cassaroli's meeting with Kadumi by Israel's foreign ministry stated that "Israel was astonished to learn that the Vatican has received a representative of the terrorist organization that claims credit for the brutal murder of innocent civilians, and has made the destruction of the Jewish state its central objective... Israel can only note with regret that this recent act cannot contribute to the peace efforts but, on the contrary, can only cause damage to these efforts."

In 1982 Arafat was neither a Nobel Peace Prize laureate nor a president. He was simply a terrorist, a butcher, a killer, the head of a criminal militia. The greatest modern assassin of Jews. The twenty-minute meeting between the Pope and Arafat took place at the papal summer residence at Castel Gandolfo in the Alban Hills south of Rome. Ciro Benedettini, assistant director of the Vatican press office, said the two men spoke of the "persistent situation of

---

[125] Ansa News Agency, 1989
[126] "Israel's outrage, pain over the relations of Vatican and PLO," The Globe and Mail, April 3, 1981

unheard-of violence that continues to mow down victims" and affect holy sites.

"Vatican says John Paul wants to meet guerrilla leader," said the Associated Press.[127] By warmly welcoming Arafat, the Pope did the PLO and its Arab League sponsor a tremendous service. The Pope's attitude toward the conflict was highlighted in a controversial speech delivered on October 5, 1980, in Otranto, Italy. "The Jewish people, after a tragic experience linked to the extermination of so many sons and daughters, gave life to the State of Israel. At the same time a sad condition was created for the Palestinian people who were in large part excluded from their homeland."[128]

The Pontiff's address was stunning in its frankness. No previous Pope had ventured to go so far publicly by linking the Holocaust to the Israeli responsibility for the plight of the Palestinians. No mention of the war of extermination of the Arab states in 1948. No mention of the real roots of the Palestinian refugees. In Vatican 'logic,' the Shoah can be compared with the Palestinian diaspora.

On March 1988, the Latin Patriarch of Jerusalem, Michel Sabbah, named by Pope John Paul II to represent the Christians in the region, accused Israel – confronted with Arab-Palestinian terrorism – of imposing measures which inflicted "the sufferings of the Passion of Jesus on the Arab Christians."[129] In 1989 the U.S. Roman Catholic Bishops criticized "long-denied rights" of Palestinians. The Ad Hoc Committee on the Middle East was made up of Archbishop Roger Mahony of Los Angeles, Cardinal John O'Connor of New York and Bishop William Keeler of Baltimore. The statement was presented to the nation's 300 bishops at the National Conference of Catholic Bishops, meeting in Baltimore. The bishops failed to give equal weight "to Israel's very real problems and legitimate rights in maintaining order in the

---

[127] Associated Press, September 11, 1982

[128] "Church and Jewish people," by J.G.M. Willebrands, Paulist Press, 1992

[129] Ansa News Agency, March 27, 1988

territories," and a 40-year history of terrorist attacks by Palestinians, said Rabbi A. James Rudin, national interreligious affairs director of the American Jewish Committee, and Judith H. Banki, his associate. The bishops said the statement was devised after consultations with the Vatican. The Catholic body called the Palestinian Intifada not a terrorist uprising, but a "cry for justice."[130]

In October of 1989, the Pope underscored again his call for a Palestinian homeland, saying, "I wish to make my own the legitimate request of the Palestinian people to live in peace in their own country." Addressing thousands of people gathered outside Saint Peter's Basilica, the Pope said that it would "be wrong to remain indifferent to such cries and to the daily sufferings of so many people." The Pope did not mention Israel in his weekly address. The Pope showed concern for a homeland for the Palestinians, but despite the 40 years of Israel's existence the Vatican had yet to recognize or show the same concern for the homeland of the Jewish people. The Pope was morally blind to the nature of the Arab-Israel conflict. By his actions and silence, the Pope condoned and legitimized Arab terrorism. He did so by repeatedly embracing the man who was responsible for introducing terrorism against innocent individuals. Arafat was always welcome in the Vatican, despite the blood of so many innocent Jews on his hands. It was Arafat who personally ordered the murder of children at play in Israeli schools, of old Jews at prayer in synagogues throughout Europe and of tourist families flying on international aircraft.

One of the terrible tragedies of the 20th century is that Arafat-inspired terrorism worked. The message of the Pope's silence was that as long as the cause is believed to be just, terrorism is an appropriate means for achieving it. The Pope was not, of course, alone in legitimating Arab terrorism. The Nobel Peace Prize Committee sent a powerful message of legitimization by including

130 "U.S. Bishops Attack Israeli Rights Abuses, Call for Palestinian Homeland," Associated Press, October 11, 1989

Arafat among its list of laureates. But one moral mistake does not justify another. And no other person in the world claims to be "the Vicar of Christ." It was right for Israel to be negotiating with Arafat, despite his terrorist past. Pragmatism demands negotiation even with criminals. But the Pope was a man of moral authority. His role was not to compromise between right and wrong. He claimed to be a believer in absolute principles of natural law and natural rights, and surely under those principles no end justifies the means of terrorism. Yet the Pope — by his silence — conveyed a powerful message that terrorism against innocent targets need not be condemned.

When Arafat died in 2004, the Vatican made stunning comments on the death of the terrorist: "At this hour of sadness... His Holiness Pope John Paul is particularly close to the deceased's family, the Authorities and the Palestinian People. While entrusting his soul into the hands of the Almighty and Merciful God, the Holy Father prays to the Prince of Peace that the star of harmony will soon shine on the Holy Land."[131] Papal representative Joachim Navarro Valls went on to call Arafat "a leader of great charisma who loved his people and sought to lead them towards national independence. May God welcome in His mercy the soul of the illustrious deceased and give peace to the Holy Land."[132]

That the world's foremost spiritual shepherd could describe himself as being close to Arafat's family, rather than the thousands of murdered Jewish men, women and children who were Arafat's victims, is an anti-Semitic act of the worst kind. That the Vatican could describe the death of a terrorist as "an hour of sadness" and call the soul of a mass-murderer "illustrious" was frightening. There is little doubt that the Pope's uncritical embrace of Arafat will be remembered as a moral imprimatur on the deliberate targeting of innocent Israeli civilians.

A few days after the meeting between Arafat and the Pope, the 9th of October 1982, Arab terrorists killed a Jewish boy, Stefano

---

[131] Catholic News Agency, November 11, 2004
[132] Ansa News Agency, November 11, 2004

Gay Taché, in the former Jewish ghetto of Rome, while 250 Jews were leaving the synagogue. All over Europe, Jewish schools, synagogues and institutions were attacked and defaced in one of the worst anti-Semitic wave since the Second World War. In Rome, in Via Garfagnana, someone left a sign saying: "We will burn the Zionists." Israel's Chief Rabbis got right in suggesting today the Pope's meeting with Arafat led to the terrorist attack on Rome's synagogue. Rabbi Ovadia Yosef, Chief Rabbi of the Sephardim, said at a memorial meeting in Jerusalem, "The leaders are responsible. The Pope gave a reception for the chief assassin and so did the President of the country" (Sandro Pertini).

Rabbi Shlomo Goren, Israel's Chief Rabbi, said in a radio interview that "the Pope's action caused a revival of anti-Semitism in Italy and in the world," adding that he was "almost certain" the terrorist attack was the result. In a statement, Israel's two Chief Rabbis called the Rome synagogue attack, "the result of incitement by the media, begun by the Pope's granting an audience to the master-butcher, the head of the PLO... He (the Pope) welcomed him with a right royal arm." According to Goren, the Papal audience was "intended to influence public opinion against the Jews."[133]

The Pope's audiences with Arafat prepared the ground for the first Intifada, which the Vatican and its envoys in the region sanctified in many ways. 2,000 Israeli civilians lost their lives because of it.

The Vatican legitimization of the Palestinian armed struggle against the Jews didn't begin with Arafat's meetings, but on December 9, 1974, one year after the Yom Kippur War. Monsignor Hilarion Capucci, the Catholic Melkite Archbishop of Jerusalem, was sentenced to 12 years imprisonment by an Israeli court. The bishop was found guilty of smuggling arms and explosive for Fatah terrorists from Lebanon into Israel, exploiting his Vatican immunity. Another clergyman, the Reverend Elia

---

[133] Jewish News Archive, October 12, 1982

Khoury, head of the Anglican Church in Ramallah, had already been arrested and convicted in April 1969 for aiding Palestinians who had planted explosives in Jerusalem.

As a Church official, Capucci held a Vatican passport and a visa de service which Jerusalem's Foreign Ministry had issued. He repeatedly crossed the Lebanese-Israeli border at Rosh Hanikra without inspection, taking advantage of his privileged position. Patriarch Maximos V. Hahim, the head of the church, condemned the arrest as a "conspiracy," and "as part of Israel's attempts to Judaize the City of Jerusalem and drive its people away by various terroristic methods."[134] The Patriarch stated that "the possibility exists that the Bishop had contacts with people the Israelis call 'terrorists,' but whom the Arabs call Fedayeen, people willing to lay down their lives to save their homeland."

Maximos went on to say that "It is possible he believed himself carrying out his duties just as did those priests who helped Jews in Europe who were victims of the Nazis. For the Israelis this is a question of culpability, but for the Arabs It is a question of heroism." Arafat declared that "Archbishop Capucci provides evidence of the facts that this revolution has extended to the clergyman." On November 19, 1974, three terrorists from the Popular Democratic Front for the Liberation of Palestine attacked an apartment in Beit Shean, Israel, and killed four Jews. The group carried communiqués demanding Capucci's release. His release was also demanded on March 5, 1975, when Fatah members attacked the Savoy Hotel in Tel Aviv and took ten hostages. The Arab Liberation Front demanded his release on June 15, 1975, during the attack on a cooperative farm in the village of Kfar Yuval. His release was demanded on June 27, 1976, by the Popular Front for the Liberation of Palestine hijackers of Air France flight from Tel Aviv to Paris. Capucci became the icon of anti-Jewish guerrillas. And the Vatican, embarrassed or conniving, stood silent.

---

[134] Near East Report, 1974

Giulio Meotti

On December 9, 1975, Archbishop Capucci was sentenced by the Israel court to twelve year imprisonment. The following day the Vatican issued the statement: "The Holy See with the deep care and lament was informed about the sentence of the archbishop Hilarion Capucci."[135] This event – according to the statement – was a serious blow aimed at the one of the oldest and most honorable Catholic communities of the Melkite Church, in which, for many years, Capucci had been the bishop. As a prisoner Capucci was allowed to say the Mass, to wear the clerical robe and to stay in a one man cell. He was visited by priests, the Latin patriarch of Jerusalem and other Catholic clergymen. On the 31st of March 1976 the patriarch Maximos V Hakim sent letters to Gerald Ford – the president of the United States, Valery Giscard d'Estaing – the president of the French Republic, Kurt Waldheim – the general secretary of the United Nations, and to Jose Barosso Chavez – the president of the International Federation of the Red Cross and the Red Crescent Societies. He informed them that Capucci had been beaten on March 15, 1976 by the Israeli guards because he had gone on a hunger strike to protest against the conditions in which he was imprisoned. Israel denied these charges. The archbishop compared his humiliation to the suffering of Jesus Christ.

On the 29th of June 1976, Capucci wrote a letter to the Pope, priests, monks, seminarians and lay persons of his archdiocese and compared the imprisonment to the arrest of St. Paul in Rome. In the letter he emphasized his Arab patriotism, the love for the Holy Land and the desire to serve "peace and justice." Paul's VI reply to the letter was sent on September 16, 1976. The Pope expressed his gratitude for the archbishop's attachment to the Holy See, his prayers and suffering offered for the Pope, and for the peace. The Pope also said that finding the way to the agreement, harmony and peace would be the great grace of God to the people of the Holy Land. Indeed, on the 6th of November 1977 the archbishop was released and deported from the Israeli territory. After that he went to Rome.

Israel's President Efraim Katzir, in response to a personal letter by the Pope, had commuted the sentence. The Pope's promise in writing that Capucci would not "bring any harm to the State of Israel," and would no more indulge in political activity, was not respected and the prelate, after he regained freedom, participated in many propaganda meetings organized by the PLO. Immediately after the release Capucci went to Rome to celebrate a mass in the presence of Libyan, Syrian and Egyptian ambassador to the Vatican: "Jesus was the first Fedayeen,"[136] Capucci declared. The Vatican never publicly condemned Capucci for his renewed terrorist activities. Not only that, the Holy See promoted the archbishop in further appointments.

In 1979 the anti-Semite Monsignor was appointed to a post by Pope John Paul II as pastoral visitor to the Melchite communities in Western Europe. In 1980 Capucci visited Teheran on behalf of the United States, to use his influence to seek release of the hostages from the American Embassy, and, at the request of the Pope, on behalf of Iran's Catholics. In 1981 father Martin Sabanegh, secretary of the Vatican's commission for relations with Islam, took part in a conference in Rome about monotheism and Jerusalem, which became a platform used to demonize Israel and the Jews. Capucci attended the event.

In 1990 Arafat was accompanied to Italy by Capucci. There, Italian friars gave the PLO leader earth from the tomb of St. Francis and asked that it be sprinkled in the Israeli-occupied territories in the hope that bloodshed there would end. Arafat prayed for peace in front of the 13th century saint's tomb in this Umbrian hill town with Assisi's Catholic bishop and Capucci. The Vicar of Assisi, Monsignor Vittorio Peri, said afterwards that at a meeting in the adjacent monastery monks gave Arafat a wooden

---

[136] "Christian Attitudes Towards the State of Israel" by Paul Merkley, McGill Queens University Press, 2001

cask with a handful of earth from the tomb of Francis.[137] It should be reminded that the PLO at that time was not even in talks with Israel. The Vatican authorities simply welcomed a terrorist organization.

Before Arafat's visit began, the Israeli embassy accused the Vatican of providing him with a "stage for propaganda" by allowing him to visit Assisi, known as a "city of peace." Later in nearby Perugia, Arafat thanked hundreds of Italian families who had donated money to support Palestinians. Speaking at a hall inside Perugia's Priors Palace, Arafat told the families: "Thank you. Today I feel born again."

Arafat then broke down in fabricated tears, bowing his head to rest on the table as the 600-strong throng packing the hall waved olive branches and chanted "Intifada, Intifada." "You have given them a new life of brotherhood and peace," he said. "For that I say in the name of these children and in the words of Jesus Christ: 'Let the children come to me'." Arafat then addressed some 7,000 people in a square, many wearing Arab headdress and waving Palestinian flags.

In 2000 Capucci was again in the headlines, when he threw stones at Israel during a visit in Lebanon. On his way to the Fatima Gate border, Capucci stopped in the town of Bent Jbail to meet with Sheikh Nabil Qaouq, a Hezbollah leader. When he reached the border, Capucci picked up a stone and hurled it in the direction of the Israeli territory. "I wish I had been with the heroes of the intifada to take part in their battle for the independence of Palestine," Capucci told reporters.[138] Again, the Vatican didn't say a thing.

On April 7, 2002 Capucci caused another tremendous outcry with his defense of suicide bombers in a speech he gave in Rome from the stage of a pro-Palestinian parade organized by the left. "Greetings to the sons of the intifada and to the martyrs who go

---

[137] Reuters, April 6, 1990
[138] National Catholic Reporter, February 21, 2003

and fight as if they were going to a party," Capucci said. "We want our land, or we will die with dignity. Intifada till victory."[139] The Vatican daily L'Osservatore Romano did not report the words of Capucci. The Italian writer Oriana Fallaci attacked the Vatican saying that "I find it shameful that the Catholic Church can allow a bishop housed at the Vatican... to take part in a protest in Rome during which he used a megaphone to thank in the name of God the Kamikazes who have massacred Jews."[140] In 2009 Capucci was again on board the Freedom Flotilla, the pro-Hamas ship intercepted by Israeli security forces during a raid that ended in bloodshed.[141] Again, the Vatican didn't condemn the archbishop. The forgotten story of this prelate of terror not only sheds a light on the Vatican appeasement of anti-Jewish violence, even when it comes from within, but also illustrates the plot of the PLO to get the support of two Popes in its struggle against Israel.

The Intifada, the Palestinian Jihad against Israel, began on 9th of December 1987, the day after an Israeli army tank-transport truck hit a minibus carrying laborers who were returning home after a day's work in Israel. Four of the passengers died immediately. However, rumors were rife that this was not an accident, but rather a cold-blooded act of vengeful retaliation by the relative of an Israeli labor contractor who had been stabbed to death on the 7th of December.

The Heads of Churches in Jerusalem published a first joint statement on January 22, 1988:[142] "We, the Heads of the Christian Communities in Jerusalem, would like to express in all honesty and clarity that we take our stand with truth and justice against all forms of injustice and oppression. We stand with the suffering and the oppressed... We call upon the faithful to pray and to labor for justice and peace for all the people of our area. And in response to the same Word of God, prompted by our faith in God and our

---

[139] Vatican Insider, La Stampa, August 14, 2011
[140] "Oriana Fallaci On Antisemitism Today," Panorama, April 18, 2002,
[141] "Gun-Running Bishop in Flotilla" by Dexter Van Zile, Camera, June 8, 2010
[142] "Jerusalem Testament" by Melanie May, Eerdmans Publishing Company, 2010

Christian duty, we have decided to call upon all our sons and daughters who are with us... to give expression to what we feel we ought to do in these ways." According to the Catholic officials, the Arabs were the oppressed, while the Jews were the oppressors.

It was a political declaration of support for the Palestinian fighters. The Heads of Churches then call the faithful to pray "for our needy brothers and sisters." In mid-1988, the entire Christian village of Beit Sahour decided to refuse to pay taxes to Israel. The Heads of Churches responded to the Israeli siege by a statement: "We who are the spiritual fathers of the people and share the suffering of those afflicted express their growing concern and call all believers to pray with them for peace and justice." And again, just as the Heads of Churches had called for concrete action to accompany words in their first statement of January 22nd, 1988, the very next day after the publication of this October 1989 statement, the three Patriarchs (Greek, Latin, and Armenian), together with the Most Reverend Father Custos and the Greek Catholic Patriarchal Vicar Monsignor Lufti Laham, organized a convoy and travelled together to Beit Sahour. The convoy was stopped by a military roadblock at Rachel's Tomb, just at the entry to Bethlehem. Undeterred, the convoy turned around and went back toward Jerusalem, then turned west and went around through Beit Jala and so back into Bethlehem, where the Heads of Churches visited the Church of the Nativity and the Latin Parish Church of St. Catherine, in each of which they prayed together.

By mid-1990, tensions were heightened by the continuing Intifada and the presence of US troops in nearby Saudi Arabia, in response to Saddam Hussein's invasion of Kuwait. The statements in support of Intifada were signed by the heads of the major Christian communities: Diodoros I, Greek Orthodox Patriarch; Michel Sabbah, Latin Patriarch; Samir Kaf'ity, President Bishop of the Episcopal Church in Jerusalem and the Middle East; Archbishop Lufti Laham, Patriarchal Vicar of the Greek Catholic Church; Yeghishe Derderian, Armenian Orthodox Patriarch; Bishop Naim Nassar, Evangelical Lutheran Church in Jordan; Basilios, Coptic Orthodox Patriarch; Archbishop Dionysios

Behnam Jijjawi, Syrian Orthodox Bishop Patriarchal Vicar; Father Carlo Cechitelli, Custos of the Holy Land. As this list clearly shows, the two most important Vatican representatives in the region, Sabbah and Cecchitelli, supported the Palestinian war against Israel.

A famous incident took place on April 11, 1990, when the Greek Orthodox property St. John's Hospice (adjoining the Church of the Holy Sepulchre) was settled by 150 Jews. Soon discovered, however, was the fact that the right of protected tenancy in the building, which belonged to the Greek Orthodox Patriarchate, had been purchased for $3.5 million by the Ateret Cohanim, an Israeli association whose declared purpose was to repopulate the old Jewish Quarter. It was then discovered that the purchase had been encouraged and supported by key figures in the Israeli government.

On April 27, 1990, all the major Christian churches in Israel and the Territories closed and rang funeral peals in protest. It was the first time that the Church of the Holy Sepulchre had been shut down in 800 years. The Vatican envoy played a major role in the decision. The leader of the Catholic US community, Cardinal O'Connor, defined the Jewish action "obscene."[143] Black flags were raised, including one atop the Sepulchre. In a show of solidarity, Muslim leaders closed to visitors the Al Aqsa mosque and Dome of the Rock shrine. Wajih Nusseibeh, a Muslim whose family keeps the key of the Church of the Holy Sepulcher, said it was the first time the doors were closed since the Crusaders were driven out of the city by the Islamic warrior Saladin in the 12th century A.D. The Church of the Nativity and holy sites throughout the country were also closed in the daylong protest. Church bells rang in somber, funereal cadence for five minutes every hour.

A Greek Orthodox priest reached to remove the Star of David from above the doorway to the building. The Catholic authorities hadn't complained when Jordanian forces between 1948 and 1967

---

[143] "The impact of the Intifada for freedom of religion in Jerusalem," Jerusalem Institute for Israel Studies, 2011

destroyed dozens of synagogues throughout the old city of Jerusalem, but they shut down their sites because the Jews took domicile in their holy city, where dozens of synagogues flourished through the centuries. Virtually all were destroyed by the Jordanians during the 1948 war and their subsequent 19-year occupation.

In 1987, the Arab clergyman Michel Sabbah was named by Pope John Paul II to the most important position of Latin Patriarch. The Palestinization of the Catholic leadership and the Christian population's identification with the terrorist Intifada increased with the involvement of the heads of the Churches in the violent struggle. In 1989 nine heads of churches in Jerusalem issued a pronouncement against Israeli policy. Among the signatories were the Greek Orthodox Patriarch and, for the first time, the Armenian Patriarch, who until then had taken a neutral approach in the Arab-Israeli conflict. The Vatican envoy Sabbah had been successful in building an international campaign to support the Arab war. In 1990 the Middle East Council of Churches, which was joined that year by the Catholic communities in the region, including the Latin Patriarchate of Jerusalem, launched a campaign which represents a Christian view that gives theological justification to the Palestinian Intifada.

Referring to the Israelis, the prayer speaks of "those who live in fear," and asks to "free them from the illusion that depriving others of their rights, or even eliminating them, will provide security or reaffirm self-dignity." This theological outlook, which sees the Israelis as oppressors and the Palestinians as martyrs, was given even stronger expression in "The Intifada of Heaven and Earth," a "Palestinian theology" published in Arabic by Dr. Geries Khoury, a Greek-Catholic priest active in promoting dialogue between Christians and Muslims. In the English summary at the end of the book, Khoury writes that "Palestine is a land which turned into heaven because the word of God was incarnate in it... and on this good earth, the Palestinian Arab people all as one rose to express through their intifada the injustice under which they live, and the deprivation of their national and human rights."

Speaking of "theological concepts that misunderstand the spirit of the Holy Bible through their fundamental, racial or political misinterpretations," he said that "this Palestinian theology is also considered as an uprising against the exploitation of the Holy Bible to justify the settlements policy." Khoury explained the "intifada of heaven" as "the uprising of heaven which aimed at supporting man in his crushing of evil and sin so as to return victoriously to the full communion with God whose bond has been broken off by the first disobedience of Adam." Identifying the coming of Jesus with the "intifada of heaven," Khoury continued by saying that "on the basis of this established faith, the Palestinian intifada gets its legality as long as it is against evil and the wicked, injustice and oppressors, and seek{s} after justice, peace, liberty and independence." Khoury compared the birth of Jesus with that of the children in the refugee camps, while "Herod is nowadays represented by the rulers of Israel." Rev. Naem Ateek was one of the authors of the prayer. Ateek thus uses the Bible to delegitimize the Jewish State by misrepresenting the Jews' relationship with God. He recycled the charge of deicide against the Jews and directed the hostility it arouses against Israel. In December 2000, he wrote that Palestinian Christmas celebrations were "marred by the destructive powers of the modern-day 'Herods' who are represented in the Israeli government."[144]

Identification by the Christian leaders with the Arab nationalist cause was most apparent in a declaration issued by a joint council of Muslim and Christian leaders that protested the establishment of the Israel-Vatican Commission charged to examine future relations between the two. The statement was read in front of the Apostolic Delegate in August 1992. The signatories, among them the Mufti of Jerusalem, the Latin Patriarch, the Anglican Bishop and the Greek-Catholic Archbishop, expressed concern that talks between Israel and the Vatican would deal with the status of Jerusalem, which they considered "the capital of the State of Palestine." They called on the Vatican to consider "historic Arab

---

[144] "Londonistan" by Melanie Phillips, Encounter Books 2007

sovereignty over the city," and they praised "the freedom of worship and preservation of holy sites enjoyed over the centuries [that was] guaranteed by [the] historical covenant of Calif Omar, [and which had been] derived from tolerance of Islam and the teachings of the messenger of peace and love, Jesus Christ."

In 1994, while the first suicide bombers were killing dozens of innocent Israelis, the Greek-Catholic Patriarchate asked Israel to release the Palestinian inmates, because "they fought for the dignity of their own people." So the Assembly of bishops, under which all the heads of different Catholic communities – Latin, Melkite, Armenian, Maronite and Syriac – launched an appeal to free Palestinians accused of terrorism. On Sept. 28, 1995, Israel and the Palestinians signed an interim agreement concerning the West Bank and the Gaza Strip, following which Israel evacuated Bethlehem, the birthplace of Jesus. On Christmas Eve that year, Arafat was enthusiastically welcomed in Bethlehem. For the first time, the Christmas' celebrations were held under Palestinian aegis, led by Arafat. At the boundary of the Bethlehem zone, mounted horsemen of the Palestinian police replaced horsemen from the Israeli police, who had escorted the Latin Patriarch from Jerusalem to Bethlehem since 1967. With hundreds of millions of faithful Christians around the world viewing the broadcast of the Midnight Mass from the Church of the Nativity, the Latin Patriarch said to Chairman Arafat, "You are blessed, and blessed is your decision to come to Bethlehem in honor of the new-born infant."

Speeches delivered by the heads of the Christian communities heaped praise on Arafat for his estimable deeds. Anglican Bishop Samir Kafa'iti described Arafat as the heir to Omar Ibn Khatib, the caliph who conquered Jerusalem and one of the most revered figures in the Muslim tradition. The Greek Orthodox Patriarch held a festive dinner for the Palestinian leader, while the Armenian Patriarch declared that he had long prayed for this day, on which the dream of Israeli withdrawal and the return of control to the Palestinians would be realized. Arafat, for his part, emphasized the Muslim-Christian alliance against the Jews. The Vatican authorities were going to build an alliance where Jews should not take part.

In his war against the Jews, Adolf Hitler instructed a group of theologians to rewrite the Bible, in a bid to remove all mention of the Jews. In 1939 a group of Protestant theologians established an institution for the "cleansing of Judaism from Christianity." Their barbaric spirit is still living on in the Palestin-olatry. The greatest obstacle for Christian anti-Semites, German or Arab, has always been Jesus' Jewishness. Protestant theologians in Nazi Germany worked hard in a well-organized effort to deny that Jesus was Jewish. Located in Eisenach — the city where Martin Luther translated the Bible — the Institute for the Study and Eradication of Jewish Influence on German Church Life published treatises arguing not only that Jesus descended from non-Semitic stock, but that his mission had been directed against the Jewish people. The lead figure was Walter Grundmann (1906-76), the seminal figure in the effort to de-Judaize Christianity and marry the faith to Nazism. Other figures at the institute similarly combined theological and political credentials; some were even bishops.

These Nazified Christians — the so-called German Christians — vied for influence in German Protestantism with liberal figures like Martin Niemoeller and Dietrich Bonhoeffer. Even Bonhoeffer's followers would have opposed Germany's "ridding" itself of Jews by sending them to death camps, yet supported the idea that German Jews had to give up their Jewishness through baptism; they shared the view that Jews as Jews were intolerable. In 1940 Grundmann and his associates published their version of the Bible, called "The Message of God." Missing from it were the Old Testament and all references to Jesus as a Jew. Like many others, Grundmann was quickly "de-Nazified," thanks in his case to recommendations by anti-Nazi Protestants more concerned with institutional coherence than with anti-Semitism. In fact, a charge was never raised against Grundmann, even as he rose to high positions in the East German Protestant Church.

The politicization of Jesus has been one of the most lethal pieces of ammunition in the Palestinian war against Israel and it was thus disseminated to the public by the highest levels of the Catholic hierarchy. Stripped of its history and identity, the State of

Israel is no more than an "imposter" which has "usurped" a name, a history and a portion of land. The spokesmen of Christian Palestinianism members of the Catholic and Protestant clergy, bishops, priests and pastors – introduced into the Palestinian system of symbols, a Christological conception rooted in the Catholic theology of the deicidal people. It is another blood libel against the Jewish people.

Theological anti-Zionism, which represents a majority current in the Catholic Church, pursues a long-term eliminationist policy. Like Nazism, the anti-Zionist policy exploits Christian anti-Semitism in Europe and strives to de-Judaize Christianity by the denial of Jewish rights. It encourages an inversion of stereotypes, in which the Israeli Jews become modern-day Roman "oppressors" humiliating the Palestinian people, whose suffering is likened to that of Jesus. Such archaic images transform Israeli self-defense into an act of "aggression" with echoes of "deicide."

At a press conference at the United Nations in Geneva on September 2 1983, the PLO head Yasser Arafat declared, "We were under Roman imperialism. We sent a Palestinian fisherman called St. Peter to Rome; he not only occupied Rome, but also won the hearts of people. We know how to resist imperialism and occupation."[145] With a conniving smile, Arafat ended with these startling words: "Jesus Christ was the first Palestinian Fedayeen who carried his sword along the road on which today the Palestinians carry their cross."

This horrible travesty provoked no public reaction from the official Churches in Geneva, including the Vatican envoy. There was a full house, but no one expressed shock, nor was there any later protestation from representatives of the Vatican or the World Council of Churches. It was not the first, nor the last time that Arafat and others would steal the symbol of Jesus, transforming the Jews of Judea into "Arab Palestinians," inhabitants of ancient "Palestine."

---

[145] "Yasser's Terrorist Jesus" by David Littman, Frontpage, November 15, 2004

In Bethlehem, where Arafat's inaugural visit in 1995 coincided with Christmas celebrations, the entire landing ceremony, reviewing of the guard of honor, and worldwide broadcast of Christmas, were all announced over the Voice of Palestine radio and television stations as if they were all part of one great sequence.[146] Arafat connected "his" Palestine to the "blessed land" with its messianic message, widening the scope of his Islamic commitment to Palestine to embrace Christianity as well, for the Christian Arabs of Palestine are as Palestinian as its Muslims, since "Christ Himself was Palestinian." This ecumenical message, which makes Islam and Christianity (to the exclusion of Judaism) the twin divine revelations of Palestine, legitimized Arafat as the protector of the Holy Places of both faiths. The Vatican was decisive in approving his strategy.

It turned the PLO and its head into the representative and partner of world Christianity, as well as world Islam in Holy Jerusalem. Thus Arafat was able to portray himself as a better universally accepted ruler of the city than the Israelis. This new garb was epitomized by the widely-reported visit by his wife Suha (a Christian who converted to Islam as a prerequisite to their marriage) to the Church of Nativity in Bethlehem with her daughter, as if to proclaim that his Islam and her Christianity were happily wed together and jointly perpetuated in the persona of little Zahwa.

According to Raphael Israeli, "his beau geste of extending his loving care to Christianity in Palestine immediately attracted the interpretation that he coveted and had probably intended." The Greek-Orthodox Patriarch of Jerusalem declared to a delighted Arafat, "Here is the successor of Sophronius welcoming the successor of `Umar ibn al-Khattab." No one present or watching on television could miss the parallel. Reference was made, of course, to the submission of the Byzantine Patriarch of Jerusalem, Sophronius, in AD 638 to the second Caliph of Islam,

---

[146] "From Oslo to Bethlehem" by Raphael Israeli, Journal of Church and State, Volume 43, Issue 3, July 2001

`Umar ibn al-Khattab (634-644), who conquered Jerusalem for Islam and put an end to many centuries of Christian rule. Until the Crusaders established in 1099 the Christian kingdom of Jerusalem, the city was to remain, uninterruptedly, part and parcel of Dar al Islam, the universal Pax Islamica.

According to Greek Catholic Archbishop François Abu Mokh, when Arafat was received by Pope Jean Paul II two weeks later, on September 15, 1983, he told the Pope that he felt at home in the Vatican, seat of the successors to St. Peter, "the first Palestinian exile".[147] During the 2011 Christmas Mass, the head of the Catholic Church in England and Wales also offered the Palestinians a powerful tool of propaganda: the comparison with Jesus' passion. "We are to be freshly attentive to the needs of those who, like Jesus himself, are displaced and in discomfort,"[148] Archbishop Vincent Nichols said during his sermon at Westminster Cathedral in 2011. "A shadow falls particularly heavily on the town of Bethlehem tonight... We pray for them tonight." It would have been more in keeping with Nichols' mission to mention the hundreds of Christians losing their lives to Islamic terrorism and oppressed by Palestinian Muslim dictatorship.

Nichols' sermon has an historical value, because now the entire Christian hierarchy in the UK, Catholic and Protestant, is part of the global battle against Israel. There is a virulent animosity towards the Jewish state in the established churches in Britain, which promulgate inflammatory libels against it. Barry Morgan, the Archbishop of Wales, compared Israel to apartheid in South Africa. "The situation resembles the apartheid system in South Africa because Gaza is next to one of the most sophisticated and modern countries in the world – Israel," said Morgan. The Archbishop of Canterbury, Rowan Williams, spiritual leader of the worldwide Anglican Communion, joined the Church of England's General Synod, which voted to disinvest Church funds from

---

[147] "Yasser's terrorist Jesus" by David Littman, Frontpage Magazine, November 15, 2004
[148] "UK Bishops came out against Israel," Israelnationalnews, December 29, 2011

"companies that make profits from Israel's occupation." Archbishop Morgan said in a lecture on the relationship between religion and violence, "Messianic Zionism began a policy of cleansing the Promised Land of all Arabs and non-Jews rather than co-existing with them." But there has been no such "cleansing" at all in the disputed territories. The only attempt at "cleansing" has been the Palestinian attempt to kill as many Jews as possible. According to Canon Andrew White, replacement theology is dominant in almost every church, fuelling the venom against Israel. As the Nazis tried to clean the Jewishness of Jesus, the Palestinian Authority is appropriating the figure of Jesus to the Arab cause as part of a larger effort to snatch the deed to the Holy Land from under Israel's feet. The PLO began to propagate a mythical figure to bolster its ties to the land: "Jesus, the first Palestinian."

Each year in Bethlehem, during Christmas festivities, Arafat then Mahmoud Abbas, have extolled Jesus as "the first Palestinian," an epithet repeated when Pope John Paul II visited the region in 2000. Speaking in a mosque in Palestinian-held Ramallah, Arafat declared, "No one will succeed in removing us from our land, including Jerusalem, and the Palestinian flag will fly from the Temple Mount and from the churches in Jerusalem." Arafat won the Vatican support in his terroristic strategy.

The Catholic priest Miguel d'Escoto Brockmann, as United Nations General Assembly President, in 2009 accused Israel of "crucifying the Palestinians,"[149] libeling Israel as an "apartheid" state, and calling for global trade and economic sanctions to be imposed on Israel. Brockmann's tirade was delivered on the UN's "International Day of Solidarity with the Palestinian People."

The appropriation of Jesus by Arafat was also widely reported as if it were the most acceptable of claims. The New York Times' Serge Schmemann led his December 24, 1996 story this way: "Fulfilling a pledge to be in Bethlehem by Christmas, Yasser Arafat declared today to a jubilant throng on Manger Square, "We

---

[149] Anti Defamation League, December 11, 2008

pronounce this holy land, this holy city, the city of the Palestinian Jesus, a liberated city forever, forever, forever." No disclaimer, wry or otherwise, noted that Jesus was a Jew born in Judea, or that he died more than a hundred years before Rome imposed the name Syria-Palestina on the area in the aftermath of crushing a Jewish rebellion led by Bar Kochba. The name change was meant to add mockery to the Jews' defeat by recalling historic Jewish battles with the Philistines. All of these events preceded by many centuries the Arab invasion and conquest. Apparently rewriting the history of Jesus, a Jew who founded Christianity, was viewed as ingratiating by Schmemann. CNN's Jerrold Kessel and Walter Rodgers both reported with similar nonchalance Arafat's expropriation of Jesus. So did ABC's Kevin Newman.[150]

When Israeli Prime Minister Ariel Sharon refused to allow the PLO chairman to travel to Bethlehem for Christmas, the Catholic clerics indicted the Israelis for their "inhumane" and "insulting" action. Yet the Vatican was conspicuously silent concerning Arafat's refusal to arrest the terrorists who murdered Israeli Tourism Minister Rehavam Ze'evi a few weeks before. Indeed, there were good reasons to restrict Arafat's travel. The facts speak for themselves. He was the mastermind of terrorism in the territories.

Thanks to the Vatican, the little town of Bethlehem was transformed into an arena from which to trumpet Arab determination to "redeem" Jerusalem and the whole of "Palestine" (Israel proper) by conquest and by blood. Meanwhile, Arab Christians living in Bethlehem have been the first to taste the PA's brand of "liberation." As soon as the PA began to occupy the town, Christian Arabs began an exodus. Hanan Ashrawi, PLO's foremost spokesperson, declared: "I am a Palestinian Christian and I know what Christianity is. I am a descendant of the first Christians in the world, and Jesus Christ was born in my country, in my land. Bethlehem is a Palestinian town. So I will not accept

---

[150] The Jerusalem Post, January 13, 1996

this one-upmanship on Christianity."[151] Thousands of Christians left after Arafat's return. Instead of protesting this ludicrous rewriting of history, some in the Christian Arab clergy — including Latin Patriarch Michel Sabah — appeared regularly in the foreign media as PLO propagandists. Arafat spoke of the "Palestinian Peter," thereby negating the Jewish identity of the apostle. Ignoring historical facts, the creation of a "Palestinian" Jesus, of a "Palestinian" Mary and "Palestinian" Apostles is pure nationalism serving a political cause. This approach feeds into the popular "Islamization" of Jesus and the entire New Testament, as if it were part and parcel of the Arab and Islamic legacy. The odious invention of a "Palestinian Jesus" persecuted by the Jews is central to the multifaceted Arab campaign that includes boycotts and terrorism, the so-called "right of return" and diplomatic attempts to isolate Israel internationally. According to this Palestinian propaganda, Jesus was not born a Jew but a Christian, and Bethlehem was not a Jewish town in Judea, but a Muslim-Arab one.

Under the PLO's dictatorship, Jewish history has already become "Palestinian Arab history" and the Jewish nation ("Am Yisrael") that ruled in the Holy Land for a thousand years and developed a world-shaking culture never existed. The brave Jewish historian Bat Ye'or in the pivotal book "Dhimmitude" called it "Arabization of Jesus" and "de-Judaization of the Bible," which are both serving the Palestinian cause. After Hitler's Holocaust which tried to destroy the body of the Jewish people and Stalin's Holocaust which tried to destroy the heart of the Jewish people, it is now the turn of the Palestinian ideological Holocaust seeking to destroy the history of the Jewish people.

Today Catholic groups such as Trócaire and Pax Christi manipulate Christmas symbols to advance boycott, divestment, and sanctions campaigns against Israel.[152] The campaign is made

---

[151] "Anglican Woman 'Making a Difference' to the World as Palestinian Spokeswoman," Episcopal News Service, February 7, 1992
[152] For the Christians' manipulation of Jesus' story, see the NGO Monitors' reports

through politicized Christmas carols, cards, and messages, and calls for donations and gift giving. Trócaire claims that a "gift of olive trees... will also support Israeli and Palestinian organizations working to promote a just and lasting peace." The Ireland Palestinian Solidarity Campaign sold a card with a Madonna and child image in green, red, and white – the colors of the Palestinian flag. The Amos Trust's Nativity Church is "complete with separation wall" depicting the "current situation in Bethlehem. It includes... a palm tree to replace the wall for a more traditional nativity scene – ideal for churches and campaigners." The association of Palestinians with Jesus' suffering invokes classical anti-Semitic tropes.

Palestinians have taken to claiming that the 3,000-year-old bond between Jews and the land of Israel is either non-existent, or is dwarfed by an even older bond linking the land to Arabs. In an interview on Qatar television, Arafat insisted that even Abraham, the Jewish patriarch, was not Jewish at all, but "simply an Iraqi." The Arab Studies Society, an arm of the Palestinian Authority, publishes an official map of "Palestine" that omits every Jewish religious site in Israel, along with hundreds of Jewish towns and villages. On this map, Eilat doesn't exist, Tel Aviv is a tiny village, and the Old City of Jerusalem becomes the Palestinian "capital." Western Jerusalem, with its half-million Jewish residents, disappears. The Palestinian Authority's television channel aired a program asserting that the tales of the Old Testament took place in what is today Yemen, not in Israel. Another PA-TV show argued that Palestinian Arabs are "the true descendants" of the biblical Israelites, not the Jews.

On Christmas 1996, just after the Israeli hand-over of Bethlehem to the PA, Arafat held a rally at the Church of the Nativity. "This is the birthplace of our Lord the Messiah, the Palestinian,"[153] he declared. "This is the holy city, the city of the Palestinian Lord." Jesus, needless to say, was a Jew, born to a

---

[153] Boston Globe, August 26, 1997

Jewish mother in a Jewish town, 135 years before the name "Palestine" was even invented, 650 years before the Arabs swept out of the Arabian peninsula to begin their conquest of the Middle East, and approximately 1,967 years before Arabs from Israel started calling themselves Palestinians.

This theme of Jesus and "Palestine" became a constant in the framework of Palestinolatry. Historian Bat Ye'or has explained this well, showing how – after the Second Vatican Council and the Nostra Aetate Declaration (1965) – the recycling of Christian religious symbols in the Arab-Muslim war on Israel was carried out at the instigation of Christian clergymen. The Christological themes of Palestinianism are based on the traditional Judeophobic schemas of the crucifixion and were introduced via the Arab Churches. The Arab Palestinian Churches transfigured the Arab Palestinian terrorist into a Christ-like image. The assassination of Jews was thus hallowed.

In 1997, at Har Homa, a stony hillside in the Judean desert overlooking Jerusalem and repopulated by the Jews during the last decade, three Christian Arabs had themselves bound to crosses at Easter to protest the building of houses on land owned by a Jew. No Vatican or other Christian authority protested with the Palestinian Authority. Probably the most heinous insult to both Judaism and Christianity occurred on December 11, 2000, two weeks before the Christmas Jubilee, ten weeks after the Second intifada began with the savage Palestinian attacks on Israeli civilians. A Palestinian daily, "Intifada," displayed on one-half of its front page a provocative caricature, showing a crucified young woman called "Palestine" – with blood flowing from her pierced hands and feet. A long spear transfixes her body to the cross, its protruding point embossed with a Star of David, and an American flag at the shaft end. Blood spurts from her martyred body down upon a trio of huddled, caricatured Oriental Jews, who are looking up and grimacing at the crucified young woman, clearly meant to symbolize Jesus and "Palestine." On December 14, Intifada went a step further. Alongside a battered cross appeared a pious prayer to "My Lord the Betrayed … betrayed by the contemptible treasonable kiss," and ending, "O Son of the Virgin, they cannot overcome you twice..."

There was no official Church reaction before or after Christmas to this gross defamation of Christianity – and of hate-propaganda against Jews and Judaism – at the close of the Jubilee Year 2000, after the earlier visit of Pope Jean Paul II to Jerusalem.

Today the Catholic pilgrims spend virtually all their time visiting holy sites in Palestinian-run territory, staying in Palestinian hotels and listening to Palestinian tour guides. As a result, people who start out on such pilgrimages in a state of almost total ignorance of Israel and the Jews return filled with hatred towards them. The Vatican bears a great responsibility in this ritual.

According to Melanie Phillips, "The real motor behind the Church's engine of Israeli de-legitimization is theology—or, to be more precise, the resurgence of a particular theology that had long been officially consigned to ignominy."[154]

This is "replacement theology," sometimes known also as "supersessionism," a doctrine going back to the early Church Fathers and stating that all God's promises to the Jews—including the land of Israel— were forfeit because the Jews had denied the divinity of Christ. This doctrine lay behind centuries of Christian anti-Jewish hatred until the Holocaust drove it underground. The ancient calumny that the Jews were the murderers of God and had denied His love thus still had resonance for Anglicans. So when Arab Christians reinterpreted Scripture in order to delegitimize the Jews' claim to the land of Israel, this kick-started replacement theology, which roared back into the imaginations, sermons and thinking of the Anglican Church.

This revisionism held that Palestinian Arabs were the original possessors of the land of Israel. The Anglican bishop of Jerusalem, Riah Abu el-Assal, claimed of Palestinian Christians, "We are the true Israel... no-one can deny me the right to inherit the promises, and after all the promises were first given to Abraham, and

---

[154] "Londonistan" by Melanie Phillips, Encounter Books, 1997

Abraham is never spoken of in the Bible as a Jew... He is the father of the faithful." According to Bat Ye'or, "Palestinian Marcionism (Palestinianism) paves the way for the Islamization of the Church as it prepares mentalities for an Islamic replacement theology." The leaders of Western Christendom have been silent in the face of Palestinian Muslim anti-Semitism and also ignore the anti-Zionist and anti-Israel propaganda of Palestinian Christians. Palestinian "Liberation Theology" is a kind of revived Marcionism.

In the 2nd century C.E., Marcion argued that the Christian gospel was the antithesis of the Torah, which reflected an evil and legalistic Jewish God. Jesus was sent by the God of goodness, whereas the law came from the God of justice. Marcion believed that Christianity had to sever itself from all things Jewish. Marcion's form of Christianity was very popular in the second century, with some scholars suggesting that for a short while there may have been almost as many Marcionite as non-Marcionite Christians. However, Marcion's view did not prevail; it eventually came to be considered a heresy, and his followers disappeared.

Palestinian clergy follow Marcion in separating the Old Testament from the New, erasing where possible words like "Israel" and "Zion." Neo-Marcionism is particularly strong within Palestinian Christianity—Catholic, Protestant and Greek Orthodox—in a sophisticated distortion of the Scriptures. Palestinian Christianity revives and promotes Marcion's teaching that the New Testament is the gospel of love and justice—whereas the Old Covenant is the "Book of Wrath and Law." Within "liberation theology," neo-Marcionism has been particularly influential with the help of highly manipulative propaganda. There is not a single Church document — Catholic or mainline Protestant — that denounces or even criticizes Palestinian Christianity's anti-Zionism. In strictly private talks, some officials in the Vatican do state their personal regret at Palestinian anti-Zionism and neo-Marcionism. But nothing is said publicly.

The process of Palestinization of the Catholic Church in the Holy Land reached its zenith in 1987, at the height of the Intifada,

Giulio Meotti

with the appointment of an Arab clergyman, Michel Sabbah to the key position of Latin Patriarch. Sabbah said that the Israeli-Palestinian conflict has unleashed "forces of evil" across the Middle East and that conflict perpetuates because of Israel's "unwillingness" to make peace. "If there's a state of one religion, other religions are naturally discriminated against." Sabbah said Israel should abandon its Jewish character in favor of a "political, normal state for Christians, Muslims and Jews." In August 2002, the Latin Patriarch met in Gaza for the first time yesterday with the founder of Hamas, Sheikh Ahmed Yassin. Sabbah then defended the Islamist terrorists of Hamas ("they protect us," he said in 2010).[155]

Sabbah's defense of Jihad against the Jews has been so embarrassing that even the newspaper Catholic Herald published an editorial titled "Why the Latin Patriarch's defense of holy war is so wrong."[156] "The militantly anti-Israel stance taken by the Latin Patriarch is reminiscent of the attitude 30 years ago of then Patriarch, Archbishop Beltritti. One of his protégés was the notorious Archbishop Hilarion Capucci, convicted of smuggling weapons into Israel for terrorist purposes. He was condemned to a long prison sentence which Israel lifted after a guarantee from the Holy See that Capucci would be removed from the area and never again permitted to engage in subversive activity against Israel. This understanding, unfortunately, was subsequently dishonored."[157]

Sabbah is an elegant man, with a degree from the Sorbonne University in Paris, who speaks fluent Arabic, English, French and Italian. While writing from within the Palestinian context, Sabbah operates within a broader Catholic context, and he has emphasized repeatedly in his writings that the church of Jerusalem joins the worldwide Catholic communion in its post-Vatican II teaching on Judaism. "In communion with the entire Church, the official

[155] "No difference between Palestinian Christians and Muslims: an interview with Michel Sabbah" by Laurent Grzybowski, 20 April 2010
[156] "Why the Latin Patriarch's defence of holy war is so wrong," Catholic Herald, February 9, 2001
[157] Catholic Herald, February 9, 2001

teaching of the Roman Catholic Church regarding the Jews and Judaism is also our teaching." Sabbah also turns to Scripture itself to insist that the land ultimately belongs not to the elect people but to God. Israel in the Bible was not the absolute owner of the land, but was "only God's guest." This is replacement theology which for centuries fuelled anti-Jew hatred all over Europe and the Middle East.

Sabbah expressed his Palestinian collaborationist sympathies most forcefully during a visit to a refugee camp near Bethlehem in 1999. The patriarch placed a wreath on a memorial to the "martyrs,"[158] whom we might call terrorists. He maintained that the right of return is "an existing fact that cannot be given up," and declared that Israel's "extracting our rights in all circumstances is a form of jihad" against the Palestinians. "Love is power and jihad does not express weakness," he told the newspaper Al-Quds.

Sabbah goes further by excusing suicide bombing as a legitimate response to Israel. Sabbah said in a 2002 videotape to Palestinian Christians: "Ours is an occupied country, which explains why people are tired and blow themselves up. The Israelis tell Palestinians 'Stop the violence and you will have what you want without violence.' But one has seen in the history of the last ten years that the Israelis have moved only when forced by violence. Unfortunately, nothing but violence makes people march. And not only here. Every country has been born in blood."

Sabbah's service to Arafat's terrorists extends beyond words. On New Year's Eve 2002, the patriarch led a "peace" march toward one of the Israeli checkpoints. Sabbah's anti-Semitism is deep and overt, as evidenced by his remarks toward Arafat during Christmas Mass in 1995. In welcoming the Palestinian leader, the patriarch "was happy to recall" how Byzantine Patriarch Sophronius tried to persuade Muslim Caliph Umar Ibn al-Khattab to prohibit Jews from living and worshipping in Jerusalem after conquering it in 636 – eight years after Sophronius instigated a

---

[158] "Patriarch of Terror," Frontpage Magazine, January 4, 2005

widespread massacre of Jews. "In the end," Sabbah once said, "we will send them away just as we did to the Crusaders."

Since 1999, Sabbah has been president of Pax Christi International, a Catholic organization that advocates radical pacifism and excusing Palestinian terrorism. Sabbah told the Pax Christi US 2003 assembly, "With the start of the second intifada or Palestinian resistance, under the guise of dismantling the infrastructure of Palestinian terrorism, Israeli forces have systematically destroyed almost every political and civil Palestinian institution over the last twelve months. Not only have President Arafat's government and security services been decimated, banks and businesses, schools and research centers, town halls, media outlets, the land registry and the courts have been violated or destroyed. A peaceful future cannot be shaped in this way."

In 2002, when the Israelis were daily attacked by the suicide bombers, Sabbah used his Christmas sermon to address the Israeli people in a very violent way: "Blood has been flowing in your cities and streets, but the key to solving this conflict is in your hands. By your actions so far, you have crushed the Palestinian people, but you still have not achieved peace." In his Christmas 2003 sermon, Sabbah criticized the security fence that helps Israel protect its citizens from suicide bombers, and called Israel's occupation of the West Bank and Gaza Strip the conflict's "basic evil." "The sacrifices of these years will not be for nothing if those responsible conclude the true results, rather than concluding that building the wall is the true solution," the patriarch said. "The true results are that war destroys people and places and does not silence a people that demands its freedom."

Sabbah reiterated the theme in 2010. "Bethlehem should be a free city," he said on December 21. "The Israeli authorities resumed the work to complete the wall, which makes Bethlehem a big prison. Ending the oppression and the humiliation of the Palestinians would at the same time put an end to the fear and insecurity of the Israelis." This canard has been successfully disseminated by Catholic prelates in the Western conscience.

Sabbah also praised Saddam Hussein, stating that "he kept in heart the Palestinian cause." "There is discrimination linked to the nature of the state; Israel says simply, 'I am a Jewish state' and that creates discrimination with regard to non-Jews," said Sabbah in December 2007 as highest Catholic prelate for Israel, Jordan, Cyprus and the West Bank-Gaza. Sabbah never demanded the de-Islamization of his native land, from which his Christian flock continues to flee en masse. According to Sabbah's racist logic, the Jews are not a people upon which a state can be built, but rather — and despite what they may say about themselves — merely a religion. Sabbah's flirting with terrorism started in 1988, when he approved the First Intifada: "History shows that rights are acquired only through violence." Let's hope that one day these prelates will be judged for the crimes they brought upon the Jewish people.

Giulio Meotti

5. THE CHURCH DURING THE "NEW SHOAH"

In 1995 the head of the PLO, Yasser Arafat, declared to a jubilant throng in Manger Square, Bethlehem: "We pronounce this holy land, this holy city, the city of the Palestinian Jesus, a liberated city forever, forever, forever!"[159] There were flags and drums, the beat mingling with songs blaring from loudspeakers and the Islamic call to prayer from a minaret. The winding streets were festooned with Palestinian flags and portraits of Arafat, while the shops displayed Christmas decorations containing the PLO leader's likeness.

Seven years later, on April 1, 2002, 200 Palestinian terrorists entered Bethlehem's church and remained inside for one month. Then began the Vatican's litmus test on terrorism against Israel. The Basilica is the second most important Holy Place for Christianity since it was built over the grotto in which Jesus was born, as it is written in the New Testament: "Mary placed him in a manger, because there was no room for them in the inn" (Luke, 2,7). The birth of Jesus in Bethlehem is linked to the fact that King David was also born in this town, and the genealogy of Jesus makes him a descendant of David (Matthew, 1,1-17). Queen Helena, the mother of Emperor Constantine, dedicated the first church on 31 May 339, but most of what can be seen today, dates from the Crusaders' renovation of the church.

Bethlehem is the epicenter of Christians disappearing after the Islamist violence. Not remarked upon by the Western media, a systematic campaign of persecution against the Christians is continuously taking place in the Palestinian areas, where the number of Christians has dropped from 15% in 1950 to just 2%

---

[159] New York Times, December 24, 1995

today.[160] It is a religious and ethnic cleansing ignored by the worldwide Churches. Since the first Intifada, the Palestinian Christians created a Muslim-Christian unity to portray Israel as the "aggressor," the "colonizer," and the "invader." Palestinian Christians thought that the Islamic-Christian front against Zionism would help secure their position in the Arab world, which is why the Arab Christians, especially the judeophobic clergy, have been in the vanguard of the battle for the destruction of Israel.

A century ago, Christians dominated the intellectual and commercial life of the Levant, comprising more than one-fifth of the 13 million people of Turkey, the region's ruling power, and most of the population of Lebanon. Nationalism opened the door of political leadership to Arab Christians. The Syrian Christian Michel Aflaq founded the Ba'ath party, which later took power in Syria and Iraq. The rise of secular Arab movements with strong Christian influence was a response to the Arab failure to prevent the founding of the State of Israel. It was a political operation which served also to cover the crimes committed against Christian brethren by the PLO and other Islamic groups: forced marriages, conversions, beatings, land theft, fire bombings, commercial boycotts, torture, kidnapping, sexual harassment, and extortion. Arab Christians were obliged to make continual compromises, afraid to mention their own suffering for fear of irritating the Muslim authorities. Soon it became a taboo subject even in the West. Bat Ye'or, the brave historian of the Jewish-Christian persecution in Islamic lands, calls this dehumanized condition, "dhimmitude."

Palestinian Christians today have to speak out against "the Israeli occupation," because, if they don't, their silence will be perceived as pro-Israeli by the Muslims. Christian leaders don't denounce the fact that they have suffered the most from the mafia-style rule of Yasser Arafat's kleptocracy, that slogans like "Islam will win" and "First the Saturday people then the Sunday

---

[160] "The Beleaguered Christians of the Palestinian-controlled areas" by David Raab, Jerusalem Center for Public Affairs, January 2003

People" have been painted on their churches, that PLO flags were draped over Jesus' crosses, that fifty years ago hardly a minaret rose above the rooftops of Beit Sahur, Beit Jallah, Ramallah or Bethlehem. After the 1948 war, Christian communities suffered most in the West Bank, not under "Israel's occupation," but because Muslim refugees were cynically settled in their midst by the Arab leadership. Thus Ramallah was 90% Christian before the war and contained 5,000 inhabitants, while Bethlehem was 80% Christian and had 9,000 inhabitants. By 1967, there were 16,000 people in Bethlehem, of whom only 6,400 were Christian, and Ramallah is a large Muslim city today.[161] In 2007, one year after the Hamas takeover, the owner of Gaza's only Christian bookstore was murdered. Christian shops and schools have been firebombed. Ahmad El-Achwal is just one of the many Palestinians who converted to Christianity, killed by Islamic militants.

In a process of "Lebanonization," Arafat changed Bethlehem's demography by incorporating thousands of Muslims from the refugee camps. Arafat then turned the city into a safe haven for suicide bombers and transformed the Greek Orthodox monastery, located next to the Church of Nativity, into his residence. Christian cemeteries and convents were desecrated and Christians became the PLO's human shields. In the first year of the Second Intifada, when Arafat's terrorists ravaged Christian towns with gunfire and mortars, 1,640 Christians left Bethlehem and another 880 left Ramallah. When in 1991, the Iraqi rockets hit Tel Aviv, Palestinians mounted rooftops and chanted: "Saddam, Saddam, ya habib, oodroob oodroob Tel Abib" ("Saddam, Saddam, you darling, hit Tel Aviv over and over again"). A few attacks later, a paraphrased version of that ditty spread around: "Saddam, Saddam, our boss, go ahead and hit the Cross."

The silence of the Vatican and the World Council of Churches has been astonishing. Only a few Christian leaders have been brave enough to denounce what is taking place in the Palestinian areas.

---

[161] "Some truths about Palestinian Christians" by Seth Franzmann, Jerusalem Post, May 12, 2009

With harsh and unexpected words, in 2005 the Custodian of the Holy Land, Pierbattista Pizzaballa, said to an Italian newspaper: "Almost every day – I repeat, almost every day – our communities are harassed by the Islamic extremists."[162]

When the Palestinian Christians approached their organizations and complained terrorists were using their houses to fire on Gilo, international Christian solidarity did not meet the challenge. The Vatican also stood silent. In 2012 the head of the Roman Catholic Church in England, Archbishop Vincent Nichols, urged William Hague, the UK Foreign Secretary, to address the "tragic situation"[163] facing Palestinians. Not because Islamists' threats, but because they were "displaced" by the Israeli barrier in Beit Jala, despite the fact that in constructing the security barrier, no land had been annexed by Israel, no houses had been demolished, no-one has been required to leave their home. In fact, the bigger truth ignored by the Western press and the Churches is that Israel's barrier helped restore calm and security not just in Israel, but also in Bethlehem.

The Church of the Nativity, which Palestinian terrorists defiled in 2002 to escape from the Israeli army, is now filled again with tourists from around the world. Also the Catholic and Orthodox Churches frequently asked the Israeli authorities to change the route of the fence. They simply didn't want to live under the Palestinian autocracy. Thus, for example, the Rosary Sisters School in the Dachyat El Barid neighborhood north of Jerusalem, was included on the Israeli side of the fence, in light of requests from the Mother Superior of the Order. Palestinian Christians today risk the same fate as their brethren in Lebanon. Everyone remembers the Phalange atrocities at Chabra and Chatila. But very few know that the first place ethnically cleansed during the civil war was a Christian town. It was November, 1976. Palestinian forces came into Damour. Palestinian fighters dynamited homes and churches, massacring entire families. They exhumed the dead from the

---

[162] Corriere della Sera, September 4, 2005
[163] The Daily Telegraph, April 2, 2012

Christian cemetery and scattered skeletons throughout the rubble. 500 Christians died that day.

Will Bethlehem be a second Damour? As it happened in Lebanon, the State of Israel has the duty to protect the Christians. When on October 13, 1990, the Syrian army, Hezbollah and other Islamic factions invaded the Christian enclave in Lebanon, only in the so-called "security zone" free Christians were able to survive. The famous "good fence" in Metulla became a symbol of cooperation and blood alliance between the Jewish and Christian peoples in the Middle East.

The threat of terrorism emanating from Bethlehem in 2002 forced Israel to defend the lives of its people and send its soldiers back into the city of Jesus' birth, which they left under the Oslo agreement. Israel desperately wanted to avert this crisis. In August, Israel gambled with the lives of its people and restored rule in Bethlehem to the Palestinian Authority, which promised to prevent terror attacks from the area. It was supposed to be a test case for the restoration of PA rule in other West Bank cities. In November came the results: a suicide bomber from Bethlehem detonated himself on a No. 20 bus in a Jerusalem neighborhood, killing 11 people aged 13 to 67. Predictably, the PA reneged on its commitment, and terrorists once again began using Bethlehem as a base to commit atrocities.

Arafat, who proclaimed himself "champion of Christian rights," allowed Christians to be used as human shields in his terrorist war against Israel. But in Vatican nobody protested against his ideology and practice. Palestinian gunmen transformed the largely Christian town of Beit Jala, adjacent to Bethlehem, into a base from which to shoot at homes in the nearby Jerusalem neighborhood of Gilo, labeled by the Vatican authorities as a "settlement."

Gilo is a special symbol of the Israeli resistance during the Second Intifada, when Arab snipers fired at Jews. Gilo was turned into another Ireland. The Jewish residents began to evacuate. Fear, rage and worry dominated their minds. Gilo was the laboratory where Palestinian terrorists sought to discover whether they could force Jews into abandoning their homes. They failed. Despite repeated pleas from Christian residents to control the gunmen, the Palestinian chairman waited long months before finally ordering his men to stop shooting. Caught in the crossfire of a seemingly endless conflict, the Palestinian Christian community faced arguably the worst crisis in its long history.

The takeover of the seventeen-hundred year-old Church which marks the birth spot of Jesus was the most momentous terrorist act during the Second Intifada. A de-Judaized Jesus was transmuted into the "first Palestinian martyr," reviving the replacement theology that Christian churches in the West have only recently, formally repudiated. In the Western media, the thirty-nine-day Israeli army siege of the Church of the Nativity quickly became a metaphorical replay of the passion of Christ.[164] Its symbolism echoed "the massacre of the innocents" by Herod. The final image of the siege in Bethlehem was not the terrorist invasion of a major Christian holy place by the Arabs, but the photograph of a Jewish tank guarding the entrance to Manger Square. The Vatican contributed its part by unfounded reprimands to Israel that recalled some of the darker strands of Church history.

One of the most important Christian leaders of the Middle East, the Coptic Pope Shenouda III, banned his followers from travelling to a Jerusalem under Israeli control, and members who flouted the ban faced ex-communication from the Church. Shenouda even went as far as instructing the clergymen of Jerusalem not to offer communion to pilgrims visiting the holy city. Palestinian leader Arafat told a packed Cairo cathedral that he would defend sacred Holy Land sites in the face of Israeli aggression and called the siege on the Church of Nativity a "crime." Pope Shenouda III said to Arafat, "All our people are with you. We ask God that he saves you from the situation you are in... we hope to come visit you there in Palestine." Shenuda met

[164] "The return of anti-Semitism in Europe" by Robert Wistrich, *Shalom Magazine*, October 2005

with Syrian President Bashar al-Assad and called for a fight to "liberate" Arab territories. In an interview on Egyptian Television Shenouda said, "The Western Churches were wrong to exonerate Jews for the crucifixion of Jesus Christ," and criticized recent statements apologizing for Christian anti-Semitism.[165] He rejected any normalization with Israel.

Visiting Beirut, the Coptic Pope told a gathering of religious and political leaders: "We refute the thesis that the Jews are (God's) chosen people because with the advent of Christianity the words 'chosen people' became obsolete. To those who stipulated the Internationalization of the holy city (Jerusalem), I answer that this would mean giving up its Arab identity... Jerusalem has been an Arab land since the 7th century." He also stated that the Palestinian Islamist movement Hamas was "doing its duty" and Arab states should help the Palestinians fighting the Israeli occupation. He then justified the Jihad: "The Jews will not leave Jerusalem through negotiations. They will leave it only through blood because of its great importance to them."

The alleyways around Bethlehem's Manger Square became the battleground between Palestinian terrorists and Israeli troops. The streets were filled with scores of cars and trucks crushed flat by tanks and armored personnel carriers. The treaded vehicles had ripped up the streets and snapped the light poles, which lay scattered.

For the Israeli people, the Bethlehem siege took place during a month filled with deadly terrorist attacks, which has been called "the Black March."[166] In March 2002, a total of 132 Israeli soldiers and civilians were killed in terror attacks. A bomb exploded near a yeshiva in the Beit Israel neighborhood in Jerusalem, killing 11; a terrorist opened fire at an IDF checkpoint near Ofra, killing 10; a suicide terrorist blew himself up at Jerusalem's Café Moment, killing 11; a suicide terrorist blew himself up on a bus near Umm el

165 "Abrahamic faiths mocked by anti-Semitic conspiracy canards" by Rabbi Abraham Cooper, Huffington Post, August 15, 2011
166 "How Israel defeated terror" by Yedioth Ahronoth, April 12, 2012

Fahm, killing 7; a suicide terrorist blew himself up in the Matza restaurants in Haifa, killing 16. And these are just the highlights. The worst massacre of Jews took place on March 27, when a Palestinian suicide bomber disguised as a woman walked into the Park Hotel in Netanya as Jews were sitting down worldwide for the Passover Seder, and blew himself up together with 30 others. The attack, which came at the height of the suicide-bombing campaign against Israel during the second intifada, prompted Prime Minister Ariel Sharon to authorize the IDF to launch Operation Defensive Shield — the taking back of the West Bank.

The gunmen inside the Christian holy site in Bethlehem were all well known terrorists.[167] Ibrahim Musa Abayat is a prominent operative of the Tanzim and serves as the head of a military cell. He was responsible for the June 2001 murder of IDF officer Yehuda Edri; the September 2001 murder of Sarit Amrani and the January 2002 murder of the American-born architect Avi Boaz; and for firing mortars at the southern Jerusalem neighborhood of Gilo. Abdallah Daud Mahmud A-Kader Tirawi was involved in the execution of multiple terrorist attacks, as well as the production of explosives and weapons smuggling, and has provided safe harbor to terror operatives. Jihad Yusef Halil Ja'ara is a Tanzim operative of the Palestinian security forces who has been continuously involved in terror attacks against both the IDF and Jewish civilians in Gilo and the Bethlehem area. He is an arms dealer who has sheltered wanted terrorists. Ismail Musa Hamdan is a Tanzim operative who has perpetrated some of the most heinous terrorist attacks including the June 2001 murder of IDF officer Yehuda Edri, the September 2001 murder of Sarit Amrani and the January 2002 murder of Avi Boaz. Nidal Ahmed Abu Galif is as senior assistant to Yehiah Damseh, responsible for the Jerusalem suicide bombings in Kiryat Yovel and Beit Yisrael neighborhoods, where entire families were slaughtered by suicide bombers. Mohammed Said Attalah Salem is a senior Tanzim operative and was involved in the planning and dispatching of two Jerusalem suicide

---

[167] "Most wanted: how Israel sees the exiles," The Guardian, May 11, 2002

bombings. Kamal Hasan Hamid Born is responsible for the financing of Tanzim operations in Bethlehem, including the purchase of weaponry and explosives. He was in direct contact with imprisoned West Bank Fatah leader Marwan Barghouti and was responsible for distributing funds to terror operatives. Ibrahim Mohammed Salem is a senior Hamas operative who was in charge of organizing multiple terror attacks.

Bassam Mohammed Ibrahim Hamud is a Hamas operative involved in the preparation of explosives and the dispatching of two Hamas terrorists to carry out a suicide bombing at Jerusalem's International Convention center. Aziz Halil Mohammed Abayat Jubran is a Hamas operative who worked with Hamud.

As Sergio Minerbi wrote in a magnificent essay about the siege,[168] "the forceful entrance of armed Palestinians into the Basilica on April 2, 2002, created an international crisis, with the Holy See becoming the leader of a world wide campaign of unprecedented verbal violence against the State of Israel which brought upon it hate and despise from a large part of Christians."

A particular detrimental role was played by Michel Sabbah, the Latin Patriarch of Jerusalem, who immediately declared that the entering Palestinians were not armed, were willingly accepted into the Church by the friars, and given asylum. In short, the Catholic authorities sanctioned the terrorists' right to use the church as a shelter. One would expect that the Catholic Church would consider the "violent invasion" a proof of the terroristic and Palestinian desecration of the Basilica by the Palestinians. Father Jaeger, spokesman of the Vatican's Custodia, declared that "when the battle started, the doors of the Basilica were closed. Armed Palestinians fired at the locks, entered the Basilica and barricaded themselves in the compound." But for more than a month all of the official uproar in the Catholic Church was addressed against Israel.

---

[168] "The Vatican and the standoff at the Church of the Nativity" by Sergio Minerbi, Jerusalem Center for Public Affairs, March 15, 2004

The L'Osservatore Romano, the official newspaper of the Vatican, wrote on April 2, 2002: "Palestinian terrorism is only a pretext," because the true objective of Israel is "to profane with fire and iron the land of the Resurrected."[169] And also: "An inhuman situation, the cry of the Pope in the public audience was for the people who without water nor food, were suffering inside the Basilica." Food nor water ever lacked to the friars. Jean-Louis Tauran, of the Vatican Secretariat of State, said that the Holy See's position included "an unequivocal condemnation of terrorism," "disapproval of the conditions of injustice and humiliation imposed on the Palestinian people, as well as reprisals and retaliations, which only make the sense of frustration and hatred grow." Again, the same moral equivalence. Pope John Paul II in his Angelus message said: "From 1967 till today, unspeakable sufferings have followed one upon another in a frightening manner: the suffering of the Palestinians, driven out of their land and forced, in recent times, into a state of permanent siege, becoming as it were the object of a collective punishment; the suffering of the Israeli population, who live in the daily terror of being targets of anonymous assailants. To this we must add the violation of a fundamental right, that of freedom of worship. In effect, because of a strict curfew, believers no longer have access to their places of worship on the day of weekly prayer."[170]

On April 2, Sabbah asked the Heads of other Churches in Jerusalem to sign with him an appeal to US President Bush saying, "We appeal to you to stop immediately the inhuman tragedy that is taking place in this Holy Land in our Palestinian towns and villages. Only this morning the Israeli tanks have reached the Church of the Nativity in Bethlehem, the City of our Lord Jesus Christ. There is wanton indiscriminate killings. Very many people are deprived of water, electricity, food supplies and basic medical needs. Many of our religious institutions have been invaded and damaged." Father Manuel Musalam, head of the Latin Church in

[169] "A ferro e fuoco la terra del Risorto," L'Osservatore Romano, April 2, 2002
[170] Angelus, August 11, 2002

Gaza at the Palestinian Authority, compared the armed Palestinians in the Church of the Nativity to Jesus on the cross: "Our Palestinian people in Bethlehem died like a crucified martyr, on the rock guarded by the Israeli soldiers armed from head to foot who have no compassion, love, life, or tolerance."[171] The Pax Christi organization chaired by Sabbah released statements very frequently. On April 5, it declared:[172] "This cycle of violence must end. Moreover we are concerned over ongoing U.S. support for the Israeli occupation, support which sustains Israel's ability to, as Pope John Paul II pointed out this week, impose 'unjust conditions and humiliations' upon the more than 3 million Palestinian people living under occupation. Israel has engaged in widespread destruction of civilian infrastructure in the Occupied Territories, subjected civilians to round-the-clock curfews, denied them access to food, water and medical services and engaged in summary executions." This is a blood libel against Israel. On April 5, the Franciscan Custody of the Holy Land, fearing an Israeli assault on the Church, declared: "The friars are not hostages; they are in their own house, in the precise place where they belong, in fidelity to their divine calling, and in obedience to the orders of their superiors." An Israeli assault would be "an extremely grave violation of the holy place, of the fundamental principles of humanity and civilization, and of precise undertakings at the level of international law."

The solution that Father Jaeger would gladly accept as "reasonable, honorable and peaceful" was that Israel let the Palestinian gunmen free to go in a "convoy to another spot of the West Bank," from where the terrorists, one should note, would be able to again kill innocent Israelis. Other Vatican officials raised the possibility that the Palestinians would quit unarmed to Hebron or Gaza in a convoy under international escort. On April 8, the Pope said, "The spiral of violence and armed hostility in the Holy

[171] "Arab Christian Clergymen Against Western Christians, Jews and Israel", MEMRI, May 1, 2002
[172] "End the Occupation, end the cycle of destruction," Pax Christi USA, April 5, 2002

Land — the land of the Lord's birth, death and resurrection — a land held sacred by the three monotheistic religions, has increased to unimaginable and intolerable levels." At his public audience on Sunday, April 7, Pope John Paul II condemned the "pitiless logic of arms" that dominates the situation in the Holy Land. Not a word against terrorism.

Father Giacomo Bini, Minister General of the Order of Friars Minor, declared that during the Second World War Franciscan monasteries gave shelter to Jews and so they should do now. The inference is clear: the Israelis are the new Nazis and the Palestinians are the new Jews. In a telephone conversation with Yosef Neville Lamdan, Israeli ambassador to the Vatican, Bini, who was the superior of the 35 Franciscan friars and four nuns confined in Bethlehem, reminded him of "the heroism of the Franciscan friars during the Second World War."[173] They risked their lives and their own religious communities to save many Jews from extermination, the Franciscan superiors reminded the ambassador. Innocent Jews trying to escape a sure death were compared to armed Islamic terrorists who should be brought to trial, while the Nazis of yesterday become the Israelis of today. Bini said that the Palestinian gunmen must be allowed to leave, in order to avoid "a humanitarian catastrophe" and "useless bloodshed."

Among the Catholic organizations, Caritas developed a one-sided political action in favor of the Palestinians. Caritas Internationalis[174] sounded a false humanitarian alarm. "Ambulances are being prevented from saving lives and even being shot at by the Israeli army. Palestinian clinics and hospitals are in need of medicines but cannot get them. There has been random shooting of civilians, including children and women, by Israeli soldiers at checkpoints. The showering of missiles on civilian areas by helicopters, bombers and tanks is causing widespread terror. Israeli and Palestinian human rights defenders

---

[173] http://www.americancatholic.org/Messenger/Aug2002/Feature1.asp
[174] Fides News Agency, April 15, 2002

are prevented from doing their work. Journalists are denied access to areas where there is fighting." Caritas also fabricated many other false allegations against Israel.

On May 1, Cardinal Roger Etchegaray was sent to Bethlehem as a special envoy of the Pope, to solve the crisis "caused by the Israeli Army siege around the Basilica of Nativity," according to a press release of the Latin Patriarchate in Jerusalem. On May 8, Sabbah published a detailed declaration: "The conflict between Palestinians and Israelis is not basically a question of Palestinian terrorism that threatens security or the existence of Israel. It is a question of Israeli military occupation that started in 1967, which provokes Palestinian resistance, which then threatens the security of Israel. Oppression and humiliations imposed upon the Palestinian people can only produce violent Palestinian reactions that threaten the security of the Israeli people and fill its soul with fear and hatred."[175] According to the distorted view of the Vatican, the only reason for Palestinian violence is to be found in the Israeli policies, which means justifying "violent Palestinian reactions" as a reaction to "oppression and humiliation." Not only that, but Sabbah justifies terrorism by calling it "resistance."

The Catholic machinery including the Pope, Tauran, Etchegaray, the Latin Patriarch of Jerusalem, the Franciscans, Pax Christi, Caritas International, L'Osservatore Romano, were all in various degrees spreading anti-Israeli propaganda. Not a word of clear criticism was said about the armed terrorists who entered the Basilica. On the contrary, Catholic officials compared the situation in Bethlehem with that of Jews persecuted by Nazis and saved by Franciscan friars during WW2.

Anti-Semitic libels against the Jews can be grouped under three headings: the blood libel, the conspiracy libel, and the economic libel. The blood libel holds that Jews entertain homicidal intentions towards non-Jews; the conspiracy libel supposes that Jews act as one unit; the economic libel supposes that Jews financially exploit

---

[175] http://chiesa.espresso.repubblica.it/articolo/7604

non-Jews. The modern Churches are reviving all those three libels: the blood libel is now in vogue with the "war crimes" charge against Israel; the conspiracy libel is self-evident in Zionist demonizing; and the economic libel is a special tool in the Christian boycott movement.

During the Bethlehem crisis, L'Osservatore Romano, the Vatican daily, in an article on the front page came to the point of accusing the Jewish state of carrying out a campaign of "extermination."[176] This is a blood libel. "Rarely has history been so rudely forced and pushed backward by a clear intention to offend the dignity of a people," declared the Vatican newspaper. "The land of the Risen One is profaned with iron and fire, and is the victim of an aggression that mounts to extermination." In 1971, against the Jewish presence in the Jerusalem reunited in 1967, the Vatican newspaper began to blame "the Judaization of Jerusalem at the expense of the non-Jewish population." Since then, "hebraization" and "judaization" became two powerful words used to isolate and minimize the Israeli right to the land and its capital. When Mahmoud Ahmadinejad at the UN forum on racism held in Geneva attacked Israel and denied the Holocaust, L'Osservatore Romano published an editorial supporting the meeting as "a turning point."

"Extermination," the word used by the Vatican newspaper during the Bethlehem crisis, was meant to demonize and deny Israel's right to defense and existence. In the same days Tom Paulin,[177] a poet, Oxford University professor and regular guest on BBC television, told Al Ahram, Egypt's leading newspaper, that American-born Jews who have settled on the West Bank were Nazis who "should be shot dead." In France, demonstrators held posters aloft saying "Death to Jews." As part of the Easter celebrations, St. John's Episcopal Church in Edinburgh displayed a picture of a crucified Jesus in Mary's arms, with both of them

---

[176] "Profanata la Terra Santa," La Repubblica, April 2, 2002
[177] "Death to Jewish settlers, says anti-Zionist poet," The Guardian, April 13, 2002

dressed as Palestinians.[178] On one side of the cross stood Roman soldiers and on the other side was an Israeli tank adorned with a Jewish star.

A deep distaste for Israel animated an important segment of Catholic intellectuals. Evidence of this animosity appeared in a very Catholic representative magazine, "Segno".[179] The director is Fr. Nino Fasullo, a member of the Congregation of the Most Holy Redeemer. The Accademia Alfonsiana of Rome, connected to the Pontifical Lateran University, belongs to the Redemptorists. In an entry dated October 8, 2003, the Catholic magazine depicted Israel as "a foreign body" nourished since its beginning by "fundamentalist ideals," moved by an "irrepressible impulse" toward occupation and colonization. Israel was described as "not only foreign, but a colonizer in the deepest sense of the word; that is, a colonizer not so much as the executor of a presumably Western dominion, but as an autonomous tendency to reproduce itself according to a logic that reinforces its foreign-ness."

The siege of the Church of the Nativity was widely presented as a "Second Crucifixion." Italian cartoonist Giorgio Forattini published in the newspaper La Stampa a cartoon in which Jesus, in the crib in Bethlehem, stares at an Israeli tank with a Star of David, wondering whether "they" are going to crucify him again.[180] The same day pro Palestinian militants wrote "Israeli murderers" on the walls of the synagogue in Siena. Jewish homes, schools, and synagogues were firebombed throughout Europe. In Denmark, a Lutheran bishop delivered a sermon in Copenhagen Cathedral likening Ariel Sharon to the biblical King Herod, who ordered the death of all male children in Bethlehem under the age of two. In Germany, Norbert Bluem, a minister under chancellor Helmut Kohl, called Israel's offensive a "limitless war of annihilation," while Juergen Moellemann, an official of the Free Democrats,

---

[178] "The impact of the Church of Nativity," Haaretz, April 24, 2002
[179] "There's a Wall of Hatred against Israel," Chiesa Espresso by Sandro Magister, November 19, 2003
[180] "Manifestations of Anti-Semitism in the European Union – Italy" by E.U. Monitoring Center on Racism and Xenophobia

openly defended Palestinian violence against the Jews: "I would resist too, and use force to do so... not just in my country but in the aggressor's country as well." From voices in the Vatican, utter indifference to the murder of Jews was coupled with the charge that the Jews themselves were committing genocide. "Indescribable barbarity" was the phrase of Franciscan officials in Rome describing Israel's attempt to arrest Palestinian terrorists who had taken shelter in the Church of the Nativity.

L'Osservatore Romano described the Israeli operation in the Territories as "barbaric acts" and "a new instrument of violence that profanes the Holy Land." The official Vatican newspaper then denounced the "relentless" Israeli campaign against Palestinian leader Arafat, who was defined as "a prisoner amidst a heap of stones in Ramallah." The Vatican daily never acknowledged Arafat's responsibility in the terrorism that killed hundreds and hundreds of Israeli civilians. Instead the Israeli policy, the Vatican newspaper argued, "if at first it seemed designed to humiliate a people, now appears designed to destroy them." In June 2002, after Israel accidentally killed three Palestinian children in a military operation in Jenin, L'Osservatore Romano wrote that "the killing of harmless babies is no more 'a tragic mistake,' but a precise strategy to annihilate people and the hope of a different future."

This is another blood libel like the ones spread by the bishops during the Middle Ages.

The Italian writer Oriana Fallaci penned a brave article for Panorama magazine to protest against the Vatican: "I find it shameful that the newspaper of the Pope — a Pope who not long ago left in the Wailing Wall a letter of apology for the Jews — accuses of extermination a people who were exterminated in the millions by Christians. By Europeans. I find it shameful that this newspaper denies to the survivors of that people (survivors who still have numbers tattooed on their arms) the right to react, to defend themselves, to not be exterminated again."[181] Fallaci's

---

[181] "On Anti-Semitism" by Oriana Fallaci, Panorama, April 18, 2002

words were a rarity in the European intellectual discourse. Most of the intellectuals, writers, journalists, cartoonists and columnists took the side of the killers of the Jewish people.

The terrorist hijacking of Bethlehem's Church quickly became the "crucifixions" of the Arabs by "deicidal" Israelis, Jews. Poor Palestinians mutate into tortured sacrificial lambs slaughtered by the "Christ-killing" people. Nothing could have been better suited to revive the most deeply entrenched Judeophobic residues in the psyche of the Christian West—organically linking the present-day suffering of the "Palestinian David" at the hands of a Goliath-like Jewish state. A cartoon appeared in the French left-wing daily Libération, entitled "No Christmas for Arafat." In the cartoon Ariel Sharon was depicted preparing a cross for Arafat, with hammer and nails at the ready. An Israeli tank stood parked nearby. The caption underneath sarcastically suggested that Arafat "would be welcome for Easter." A similar motif had appeared in the Swedish newspaper Aftonbladet, whose editorial page fiercely condemned Israel's policy toward the Palestinians under a banner heading: "The Crucifixion of Arafat."[182]

The liberal Swedish Expressen identified Israel's military actions with Old Testament "vengefulness," deploring its acts of war for expressing the primitive Biblical teaching of "an eye for an eye, a tooth for a tooth." The Anglican Church Times was no less explicit in disparaging Israel's "inhumanity." The Church Times chose to mark Britain's Holocaust Memorial Day with a particularly malevolent article by the Reverend Richard Spencer, who described events in Bethlehem as a "suffering and deprivation that I could only imagine in Auschwitz." In this horrible inversion of roles, the Jews were once again chosen by the Christian authorities as the scapegoat.

The enduring image of the siege in Bethlehem has not been classified as the sacrilegious invasion of a major Christian holy place by armed Palestinians, but by the photograph of one

---

[182] "Jews in Sweden are afraid to be known as Jews," Haaretz, February 10, 2004

intrusive Israeli tank guarding the entrance to Manger Square. Worse still, Arafat, supported by the Catholic authorities, could pose as the defender of the "Holy Land." The siege of the Church of the Nativity turned into the most important Palestinian propaganda victory. The Vatican contributed its part by unfounded reprimands to Israel that recalled some of the darker strands of Church history.

During the Bethlehem crisis the Vatican raised many times the question of the holiness of religious shrines. But the same Catholic Church never raised its voice against Arab violence upon Jewish shrines and pilgrims.[183] Jews praying at the Western Wall have been evacuated on numerous occasions due to stoning attacks by Arab youths. In October 2000 Joseph's Tomb, one of Judaism's most holy site, was attacked and burnt out by a Palestinian crowd. There was a tragic aftermath. A Rabbi (Hillel Lieberman) who was watching the burning of the tomb from a nearby hillside, was shot dead by Palestinian gunmen. His funeral cortege was shot at and stoned by Palestinians. In October 2001, on the Jewish festival of Tabernacles, Jewish women at prayer at the Cave of the Patriarchs in Hebron were shot at. Several women were injured. On 19 August 2003 a Hamas suicide bomber boarded a crowded bus and detonated his bomb, packed with ball-bearings, as the bus was passing through Jerusalem's Beit Yisrael neighborhood. 22 passengers were killed, including 6 children and a mother of 13 children. It was roughly the equivalent of a suicide bombing of pilgrims leaving the Vatican, or worshippers departing from Westminster Abbey in London.

On the 17th of January 2002, a Palestinian burst into a bat-mitzvah party for a 12 year old girl in a banquet hall in the Israeli town of Hadera. He opened fire with an M-16 assault rifle, killing 6 people. On the 2nd of March 2002, a suicide bomber attacked a crowd of people who had been attending a bar-mitzvah gathering at the end the Sabbath in the Beit Yisrael religious quarter of

---

[183] "A New Shoah. The Untold Story of Israel's Victims of Terrorism" by Giulio Meotti, Encounter Books, 2010

Jerusalem, killing 11 people and wounding over 50. On the 8th of March 2002 a Palestinian burst into the study hall of a Talmudic and pre-military training college in the settlement of Atzmona in the Gaza Strip and opened fire, killing five 18 year old boys taking part in a late night Biblical study group. On the 27th December of 2002 two Palestinians infiltrated the settlement of Otniel on the Friday night and shot dead four students who were preparing to serve the Sabbath evening meal at Otniel's college of Torah studies. In March of 2002 two elderly men walking to synagogue in Netzarim were stabbed to death by a Palestinian infiltrator. On the 27th of April 2002 a Palestinian gunman infiltrated the Jewish settlement of Adora on the Sabbath night, shot four residents dead, and wounded several others. Victims included a five year old girl shot dead in her bed.

On Friday afternoons, the Machane Yehuda market in Jerusalem attracts thousands of citizens who stock up with fruit and vegetables, wine, and other last-minute provisions for the Jewish Sabbath. On the 12th of April 2002, a Palestinian suicide bomber attacked the market two hours before the Jewish Sabbath, killing 6 people and wounding 80. On the 8th of June 2002, terrorists infiltrated the settlement of Carmei Tzur near Jerusalem on the Sabbath late at night, and shot three Israelis dead, including a husband and his nine-month pregnant wife.

On the 15th of November 2002, Palestinian gunmen ambushed guards walking behind a group of Jewish worshippers returning home from the Cave of the Patriarchs in Hebron following Sabbath evening prayers. The gunmen also shot Israeli army soldiers and Hebron security volunteers who attempted to rescue the Israeli victims. 12 Israelis were killed. A defining moment in this chronicle of violence against Jewish religious life came on the first night of Passover 2002. The Passover meal is the most widely observed festive occasion of the Jewish year – a moment of togetherness, hope, and prayer for the redemption of the Jewish people. On the 27th of March a suicide bomber walked into the dining hall of the Park Hotel in Netanya and blew himself up, killing 30 Israelis who had just sat down to take part in the

Giulio Meotti

Passover meal. This is roughly the equivalent of bombing a Christmas lunch, or a Thanksgiving dinner in the United States.

Again, the Jews have been forsaken by the Catholic Church. Where was the Vatican during these massacres?

During the 1967 war, when Israel faced annihilation from the Arab states, the Vatican gave the order: "Cheer for the other side." Catholic contribution to civil discourse consisted in comparing the Israeli quick victory to the Nazi "blitzkrieg." In 1967 the National Conferences of Catholic Bishops and the National Council of Churches, the two major official Christian bodies of the United States, weren't able to issue a declaration of support to Israel's right to exist and to defend itself. L'Osservatore Romano, the official daily of the Vatican, while Israel was under attack, called for the internationalization of Jerusalem.[184]

On January 15, 1973, Israeli Prime Minister Golda Meir was received in a private audience by Pope Paul VI.[185] At the end of the same year, after the Yom Kippur war during which Israel was attacked by Syria and Egypt and risked a new genocide, the Pope dedicated most of his yearly message of December 21 to the Middle East. The Pope spoke about the hundreds of thousands of Arab refugees "living in desperate conditions"; even if their cause "has been endangered by actions that are repugnant to the civil conscience of the peoples and are in no case justified, it is a cause that demands human consideration and calls with the voice of abandoned and innocent masses for a just and generous response." No word was made by the Vatican about the impending Holocaust on the Jewish people during the Yom Kippur War.

During the Gulf War in 1991, Pope John Paul II only protested after 19 Iraqi scuds had fallen on Tel Aviv and millions of Jews had to wear the gas masks inside their own houses. The Holy See published a long document on the issue of the diplomatic relations

[184] "Christian Reactions to the Middle East Crisis: New Agenda for Interreligious Dialogue" by Judith Banki, American Jewish Committee, 1968
[185] "Vaticano e Israele dal secondo conflitto mondiale alla Guerra del Golfo" by Silvio Ferrari (1991)

with Israel. It stated that the lack of diplomatic relations is certainly not due to theological reasons, but to juridical ones. The three main difficulties were: the presence of Israel in the "occupied territories," Israel's annexation of Jerusalem, and the situation of the Catholic Church in Israel and the territories.

On March 6, 1991, Pope John Paul II closing the synod of Bishops from the Middle East, said, "We have spoken of the Holy Land where two peoples, the Palestinian and that of the State of Israel, have been engaged in conflict for decades; the injustice of which the Palestinian people is a victim, demands an engagement by all men." Saddam Hussein's scuds on the Jews, who had to wear gas masks weren't a good reason to raise the Pope's voice in the world. The World Council of Churches, the Pope, the peace activists — all who decried the U.S. and U.N. forces' attack on military installations in Iraq, were strangely silent when Israel was attacked. The World Council of Churches also tried to blame the existence of Israel as one of the "root causes" of the struggle with Iraq.

When the first of Saddam's Scuds landed on Israel, the Pope condemned attacks "on civilians" without even mentioning Israel by name.[186] Jewish leaders complained, and on January 26th hundreds of Jews with Israeli flags assembled in protest beneath the pope's balcony. The Jews, many wearing skullcaps, displayed placards proclaiming "Israel Will Not Die." The Pope's traditional blessing was drowned out by chants of "Israel, Israel, Israel" from the demonstrators, who included survivors of Nazi concentration camps. The moral blindness to terrorism and the anti-Jewish hostility has been displayed by the Vatican during all the last major wars in the Middle East.

During the Israel-Hezbollah war of 2006, the Vatican issued statements about Israeli response to the acts of aggression by terror groups, emphasizing only Israeli use of force and its impact on civilians — not the Arab terrorism and aggression that

---

[186] New York Times, February 7, 1991

precipitated the crisis. In short, Israel has been demonized on the unintended consequences of efforts to protect its citizens, while Hamas and Hezbollah have been given by the Vatican, a pass on their openly-stated goal: the destruction of the Jewish State.

The same day Benedict XVI invoked Our Lady of Mount Carmel, "the mountain in the Holy Land just a few kilometers from Lebanon, which towers over the Israeli city of Haifa,"[187] and it was upon that very city – and upon Nazareth – that rockets were launched by Hezbollah, the Lebanese terrorist militia that is an armed extension of Iran, whose strategic objective is that of wiping Israel out of existence. The Pope prayed to Our Lady of Carmel before the Angelus of Sunday, July 16 2006, from the mountains of Les Combes where he was on vacation. And after the Angelus, he summarized as follows the Holy See's view of the war that has been reignited along the Lebanese border: "At the origin of these devastating confrontations there are, unfortunately, objective situations of the violation of law and justice. But neither terrorist acts nor retaliation can be justified, especially when these come with tragic consequences for the civilian population."

In the first year of his pontificate, the only time the Pope has alluded to the intention to destroy Israel – as expressed by Iranian president Mahmoud Ahmadinejad – was in this passage of his address to the diplomatic corps on January 9, 2006: "In the Holy Land, the state of Israel has to be able to exist peacefully in conformity with the norms of international law; there, equally, the Palestinian people has to be able to develop serenely its own democratic institutions for a free and prosperous future." Not so much about the ongoing threat of a new Holocaust pending on the Jewish people.

These constant features of Vatican geopolitics all appear in the "declaration" released on July 14 by cardinal Angelo Sodano, the Vatican's foreign minister, or secretary of state: "As in the past, the Holy See also condemns both the terrorist attacks of the one and

---

[187] "Israel is fighting for his life, but the Vatican 'deplores'" by Sandro Magister, Chiesa Espresso, July 19, 2006

the military retaliation of the other. In fact, the right of a state to defend itself does not exempt it from respecting the norms of international law, especially in those matters concerning the protection of the civilian population. In particular, the Holy See deplores the attack on Lebanon, a free and sovereign nation, and confirms its closeness to the people of Lebanon, who have already suffered so much in the defense of their independence."

Further proof is found in the enthusiasm with which the official Hezbollah media outlet, Al Manar, greeted the July 14, 2006 declaration from Sodano, taking it as the position of pope Benedict XVI, "a defender of human rights and a model of sanctity." The Vatican always mired in a paradigm equating, on the one side, terrorist actions by Islamist fanatics who view both Jews and Christians as "infidels" and seek Israel's destruction with, on the other side, Israel's right to defend itself and eliminate the threats to its citizens.

During the days of the 2009 Christmas celebrations, Benedict XVI spoke out repeatedly against the Israeli war centered on Gaza. The authorities of the Church, and Benedict XVI himself, have raised their voices in condemnation of "the massive violence that has broken out in the Gaza Strip in response to other violence," only after Israel began bombing the military installations of the terrorist movement Hamas. Not before. Not when Hamas was launching rockets every day against the Jews in the surrounding area. About Hamas and its vaunted "mission" of wiping the Jewish state from the face of the earth, about Hamas as an Iranian outpost in the Middle East, the Vatican authorities have never raised the red alert.[188] They have never shown that they see Hamas as a deadly danger to Israel.

In the December 29-30 issue of L'Osservatore Romano, a front-page commentary by Luca Possati, checked word by word by the Vatican secretariat of state, claimed that "for the Jewish state, the only possible idea of security must come through dialogue with

---

[188] "In Gaza, the Vatican raises the white flag," by Sandro Magister, Chiesa Espresso, January 4, 2009

all, even those who do not recognize it."[189] Read: Hamas. And in the same issue of the Vatican newspaper – in a statement also approved by the Secretariat of State – the Latin patriarch of Jerusalem, Fouad Twal, after decrying Israel's "disproportionate" military reaction, reiterated the same concept: "We must have the humility to sit at the same table and listen to each other." Not a word about Hamas, the suicide bombings and the rockets fired on Israeli cities.

In January 2012, eight Catholic bishops from Europe and North America, including UK Archbishop Patrick Kelly and French Archbishop Michel Dubost, visited Gaza. "I asked prisoners in the largest prison in Europe (in Evry) to pray for you,"[190] Dubost told Gazans. According to the Catholic officials, the inference is clear: Palestinians are living in a big prison terrified by Israel. In the same weeks, Father Manuel Musalam, head of Gaza's Catholics, met with Hamas leader, Mahmoud al Zahar, and declared that "Christians are not threatened by Muslims" but that everyone faces the same problem, that of Israel's "humiliation." Meanwhile Maronite Patriarch Beshara Rai,[191] head of Lebanon's Catholic Church, sent his envoy, Father Abdo Abou Kassem, to Teheran for a conference in support of a "Zionist-free Middle East." The conference was also attended by Hezbollah ideologue Mohammad Raad and by Hamas leader, Khaled Mashaal.

The problem is that the "temporariness" of the state of Israel is an idea shared by the largest part of the Catholic Church. And it is this idea that influences Vatican policy on the Middle East.

In 2005, Pope Benedict condemned a litany of terrorist atrocities around the world, while avoiding mention of the 57 Israelis killed that year during the Second Intifada.[192] "Not every attack could be followed by an immediate public condemnation,"

---

[189] http://www.vatican.va/news_services/or/or_quo/commenti/2008/302q01b1.html
[190] "Bishops tell Christians of Gaza: 'You are not alone'," Christian Today, January 10, 2012
[191] "Chiesa, relazioni pericolose," Lettera 43, October 5, 2011
[192] "Pope's prayer omits Israel, and words fly," New York Times, July 26, 2005

the Vatican said after Israel's criticism of the Pope's silence. "There are various reasons for this, among them the fact that attacks against Israel were sometimes followed by immediate Israeli reactions not always compatible with the norms of international law. It would, consequently, have been impossible to condemn the former and remain silent on the latter."

In its comments, the Israeli Foreign Ministry declared, "we expected the Pope would criticize terror against Jews when deploring terror that affected others." The ministry also asserted, dramatically, that "the Pope's evasion cannot be interpreted as anything but justifying terror against Jews," and that "this can only strengthen the hands of radicals and offer them encouragement." First, the Vatican is making a clear moral equation between the murder of innocent Israeli civilians and Israel's attempts to fight terrorism. Second, it asserts the right to determine the legality of Israel's actions and to assume, a priori, that Israel's reaction to a terrorist attack will itself be "illegal." Third, the Church ignores the possibility, as in the case of the most recent attack in Netanya and many others, that Israel may not retaliate at all.

The Vatican knew Netanya witnessed in 2002 the worst terror attacks Israel experienced in its existence. A Palestinian Arab suicide bomber entered a hotel favored by devout, elderly Jews and known to be where Holocaust survivors had gone with their families for the Seder. It is the location of those mere six miles that separate Netanya on the coast from Tulkarem inland. There is an Arab saying about Netanya, alluding to it as the narrowest and most exposed throat of Israel: "When we hang you, we will hang you from Netanya." There was an enormous pool of blood, the blood of innocent Jews who just wanted to celebrate Passover together that night. A copy of the Haggadah and a piece of unleavened matzo bread were immersed in the blood. Most of the victims, many of them Holocaust survivors, were maimed beyond recognition, making it impossible to establish identity by fingerprints or birthmarks, scars or Holocaust tattoos. Why did the Vatican stand silent about this mini Holocaust; this terrorist campaign?

The last two Popes, John Paul II and Benedict XVI, both severely undermined Israel's security policies against terrorism by demonizing the security fence, which saved thousands of innocent lives, Jews and Arabs alike. "The Holy Land doesn't need walls, but bridges," John Paul II proclaimed in 2004, while the Palestinian suicide bombers were still able to penetrate into

Israeli cities to kill innocent people. In 2009 Pope Benedict condemned again the security barrier, despite the fact it had proven its efficiency in stopping the suicide attacks. "Towering over us, as we gather here this afternoon, is a stark reminder of the stalemate that relations between Israelis and Palestinians seem to have reached – the wall," the Pontiff said.[193] "In a world where more and more borders are being opened up to trade, to travel, to movement of peoples, to cultural exchanges, it is tragic to see walls still being erected."

In an interview for the Italian daily Corriere della Sera, Nobel Peace Prize and Holocaust survivor Elie Wiesel slammed the Pope's words on the barrier.[194] "I expected something quite different from the spiritual leader of the one of the world's greatest and most important religions. Or (at least) a declaration condemning terror and the murdering of innocent people, without mixing in political considerations," Wiesel said. During a Sunday's Angelus, the Pope confirmed that the "construction of a wall between Israelis and Palestinians is seen by many as an obstacle on the road toward living together in peace. Indeed, the Holy Land does not need walls, but bridges! Without reconciliation of souls, there can be no peace." Fr. David Maria Jaeger, the Israeli Franciscan spokesman for the Custody of the Holy Land commission, defined Wiesel's words as "embarrassing" and advised him to "seek forgiveness."

In 2003 Cardinal Roger Etchegaray, who has handled several delicate diplomatic assignments for the Holy See, said that the

---

[193] "Pope calls for Palestinian state," BBC, May 13, 2009
[194] "Wiesel: condanni i terroristi, non faccia politica," Corriere della sera, November 15, 2003

barrier "inevitably creates a geography of apartheid, which provokes rather than controls violence."[195] "Apartheid" has become a potent term for demonizing Israel, since it evokes the precedent of sanctions against the white regime in South Africa. The analogy is very dangerous. If it sticks, Israel's ability to defend itself diplomatically and militarily will be severely weakened. The apartheid theology dictates that all the Israeli land must be returned to Islamic rule, by force if necessary.

The security fence has been defined "humiliating and distressing" by Cardinal John P. Foley, grand master of the Knights of the Holy Sepulcher. Foley has been just one of many US Catholic leaders who questioned the security barrier. Addressing the 2010 Synod of Bishops on the Middle East, Foley falsely alleged that "the continued tension between the Israelis and the Palestinians has contributed greatly to the turmoil in all of the Middle East and also to the growth of Islamic fundamentalism."

In April 2012, the head of the Roman Catholic Church in England and Wales, Vincent Nichols, urged the UK Foreign Secretary to address the "tragic situation" facing Palestinians displaced by the building of the Israeli security barrier in Beit Jala, a predominantly Christian town a little over a mile from the Church of the Nativity. Archbishop Nichols said the "expropriation" of land by Israel had a "catastrophic impact" on the village and risked furthering the conflict. "Unfounded allegations," was the reply of the Israeli embassy. In constructing the security barrier, no land has been annexed, no houses have been demolished, and no-one has been required to leave their home. It doesn't matter, the Vatican officials just need to demonize Israel to maintain a high pressure on the Jewish State.

Defending the barrier, Israel argues that half of all Israeli civilian deaths in 2004 were caused by Palestinian suicide bombers coming from Bethlehem. Why don't these facts affect the Vatican's policy? Only a small part of the fence is a concrete wall. It is high to

---

[195] "Vatican cardinal condemns Israel's 'security wall'," Catholic World News, November 14, 2003

protect the Israeli civilians from the sniper fire they suffered during the Intifada. In 2004 the Israeli Supreme Court, which has never been tender with the Israeli governments, decided that "the fence is motivated by security reasons." The barrier has been a tremendous success, as terrorist attacks inside Israel has dramatically fallen. General Moshe Kaplinsky, who was IDF Deputy Chief of Staff, declared that "where the barrier is in operation, no terror attack goes though it. Period." Crossing the barrier is often a hard experience for the Palestinians, but what about the lives of innocent Jews killed en masse by the Palestinian suicide bombers? What's worse; being late at work or blown up by a "martyr"? The barrier has been a humanitarian way of dramatically reducing the violence — as did the IDF operations inside the Palestinian cities — and has consequently improved the security of ordinary Israelis.

In 2004 Father Marco Malagola, delegate of the Justice and Peace Commission of the Custody of the Holy Land, spoke on Vatican radio about the impact of the barrier on the daily lives of Palestinians. He called it a "permanent hell," a "lifeless existence,"[196] and said that "building this wall can only crush any hope Palestinians have. Far from being a security wall, it simply fuels their sense of hopelessness." Malagola then said that the Israelis killed and maimed forever by Arab suicide bombers are suffering less than the Palestinians. "All these suicide bombers who blow themselves up in buses, restaurants, discos engender an enduring sense of fear. However, if I had to say who suffers the most, it is those who live divided and separated under a brutal occupation. There are times when people have to wait for hours at a checkpoint only to be told they can't cross. It is a lifeless existence." Do Malagola's words deserve an explanation?

Today there are some 50 barriers and fences in the world. Bill Clinton, who came to power promising "a bridge to the 21st century," gave the US the wall with Mexico; Spain built fences to

---

[196] Asia News, July 8, 2004

keep out Moroccans; India is walling off Kashmir and Bangladesh; South and North Korea share the most heavily fortified border in the world. Elsewhere, Saudi Arabia has an epic wall project; the glitzy, wealthy Arab sheikhdoms are closing the border with dirt-poor Oman; Russia is considering walling off Chechnya; Western Sahara has "the Wall of Shame"; Cyprus is entirely divided by walls; Belfast is a fenced city of brick, iron and steel barriers, and even the ultra-liberal Netherlands built a fence around the Hook of Holland.

But only Israel's barriers have been condemned by the International Court of Justice, only Israel's fences have received round-the-clock coverage on CNN and front page stories on the New York Times, only Israel's checkpoints are turned into meccas for "peace" activists, and are condemned by Western public opinion as an instrument of harassment used to subjugate a proud "native" people, whose only crime is wanting freedom, or "liberation." Only Israel's barrier was subjected to the Vatican's moralistic and hypocritical attacks.

While foreign fences keep out livestock and refugees from neighboring countries, only Israel's fences and checkpoints have a truly humanitarian reason: to secure the civilian population's right to life. Only in Israel barbed wire, patrol roads, sand tracking paths, video cameras and electronic sensors are used to prevent a restaurant, a shopping mall or a hotel from being turned into carpets of human bodies. Paradoxically, barriers have been anathema to Jews since 1179, when the Vatican Council established the medieval ghettos throughout Europe. Yet very soon, the Jewish State will be enclosed by steel and concrete. Israel is erecting another fence to protect its civilian population from terrorist fire. After Judea and Samaria, the Golan Heights, Gaza and the Egyptian border, It is the turn of Metulla, the northern city hit by Hezbollah rockets, and where Yasser Arafat's killers murdered tourists and students. Prime Minister Benjamin Netanyahu's government removed several roadblocks in the territories to ease Palestinian daily life. It is a difficult decision, as in the past Israelis have been killed after checkpoints were removed. Since 2008, Israel removed some 30 checkpoints throughout the territories, leaving 11, mostly located along the Green Line.

None of the other fenced countries have infiltrators with the "holy" purpose of killing people. Tijuana, the symbol of the wall dividing US and Mexico, is not Qalqilya, a Palestinian city 15 kilometers from Tel Aviv, ringed by a fence and checkpoints. It is Qalqilya, not Tijuana, that has been called the "Paradise Hotel," because the city was used by suicide terrorists as the jumping off point into Israel. It is from Qalqilya, not Tijuana, that terrorists can bomb Tel Aviv's Azrieli towers, which can be seen from the city's hills. The checkpoints, Israel's most common barriers, are its most vital and disruptive counterterrorism instrument. Unlike Checkpoint Charlie in Berlin, which today is a monument to oppression's defiance, Israel's checkpoints are a symbol of life. According to the IDF, some 30% of Israel's counterterrorism arrests took place at these roadblocks.

Israel improved the quality of life at the checkpoints with bathrooms and shaded areas. But Palestinian terrorists then deliberately took advantage of it. In 2004 a Palestinian woman killed four Israelis at a checkpoint in Gaza by pretending to be disabled. Because of her condition, the soldiers performed their security checks without first using a metal detector. She then detonated her explosive device. Explosive belts and bombs are regularly detected at the checkpoints, but Western media outlets usually don't report it. Today It is only because of these symbols of security that Israelis are no longer assailed by suicide bombings and shootings like they were during the height of the second Intifada. We can draw the same lesson from the embassies' metal detectors, Ben-Gurion Airport's strict security procedures, the guards at the entrance to Tel Aviv's shopping malls, the so-called "apartheid wall," and the nuclear plant in Dimona. If the Arabs disarm, there will be peace; but if Israel disarms, there will be another Holocaust.

By repeatedly condemning the security barrier, the Vatican betrayed "The Fundamental Agreement," the accord signed by the Vatican and Israel in December of 1993, normalizing relations between the Holy See and the Jewish state. Archbishop Pietro Sambi claimed the fence violated the Fundamental Agreement. A closer look, however, does reveal a violation of the accord, but not by Israel. The Fundamental Agreement, Article 3, section 2, states that Israel "recognizes the right of the Church to carry out its religious, moral, educational and charitable functions and to train, appoint and deploy its own personnel in its own institutions for the said functions to these ends." Archbishop Sambi stated Israel is contravening this section of the Fundamental Agreement with the anti-terrorism fence. However, the next sentence is essential to understanding the previous one. It states that the Church "recognizes the right of the State to carry out its functions, such as promoting and protecting the safety and welfare of the people."

In other words, the Church can go about her spiritual duties, but she might be inconvenienced when the Jewish State attempts to protect its citizens from being picked off by snipers or blown up by suicide bombers.

Giulio Meotti

6. NAKBA AND HOLOCAUST

When Vatican officials accuse Israel of Nazi-like behavior towards the Palestinians, they are not simply saying that Israel's policies are wrong; they are assuaging their feelings of guilt and excluding the Jewish State from the family of nations. As they see it, the Jews were granted sovereignty in response to the Holocaust, but if they act like Nazis, they forfeit this right.

Sovereignty is transferred to their victims, the Arabs, and the Jews revert to their "normal" status as exiles. The interpretation of Israel as an "injustice" and as historical redress for a crime committed against the Jewish people – robbed of its identity, history and human rights – transformed the re-humanization of the Jewish victim into a conceded favor, with the implication that this favor is "temporary." It is a favor that Israel, the victim of this crime, must seek through pardon and which implies that its independence is an error which justifies condemnation.

The Nazi-Israel comparison doesn't affect only the Catholic Church. In 1991 Bishop C. Charles Vache of the Episcopal Diocese of Southern Virginia said the Israeli treatment of Palestinians "approaches genocide of the type which Jews experienced in the late '30s and early '40s in Germany." According to the French intellectual Shmuel Trigano, the Holocaust has become for the Church "the counterweight to the recognition of the Jewish condition in politics and history, namely the recognition of Jews as a people, with Israel and Zionism."[197] On this level the political beneficiaries of the memory of the Shoah are the Palestinians. "A condition that assigns a role as sacrificial victim to the Jews."

---

[197] "La nouvelle politique du Vatican" by Shmuel Trigano, controverses.fr, May 12, 2009

Across the European Union, it has become commonplace to declare that "the Jews, once victims, have become executioners." This remark of France's most popular Catholic priest, the late Abbé Pierre, was made as far back as 1991. From that time, Abbé Pierre did not tire of repeating the canard that the Jews invented genocide; that their Torah is legalistic, tribal, and punitive; and that Zionism is a vicious example of the ravages inflicted by capitalist globalization on the "wretched of the earth."

The Catholic icon Abbé Pierre was known for decades as "the champion of the homeless." He has been called "a modern Saint Francis of Assisi" and "the most famous French priest." L'Abbé Pierre, or "Priest Peter," according to French President Jacques Chirac, "was our conscience, the incarnation of goodness." In April 1996, a Marxist philosopher, and old friend of Abbé Pierre, Roger Garaudy, wrote a book suggesting that Israel had invented the extent of the Holocaust and had, in any case, exploited the suffering of European Jews to justify ill-treatment of the Arabs. Abbé Pierre defended the book.[198] He said the Holocaust, even if "mathematically" smaller than generally accepted, was an "abomination" but he could not justify the "suicidal" policies of the Israeli government. In an interview with the daily Le Matin, the French priest said that, "there weren't six million of victims because of Hitler, there were five million." Then he talked about Joshua bin Nun, the Biblical Jewish leader: "He killed everybody and everything, we assisted to a Shoah before the Shoah." Abbé Pierre's meditations at Yad Vashem in Jerusalem were symmetrically balanced by a visit to Arafat in Gaza, where he begged forgiveness for the West's creation of the State of Israel.

Two Popes did the same when they visited the holy land. On May 7, 1949, while the Jews were defending their beleaguered state, the Vatican news agency Fides ran a radical attack on Zionism, calling it "the new Nazism." The article, entitled "Christianity in

---

[198] Le Nouvel Observateur, January 22, 2007

front of the Holy Land's drama," was reprinted by La Civiltà Cattolica, the semi official Vatican magazine.[199]

A pilgrimage to Israel by the 27 top Catholic bishops from Germany in 2007 was meant to be a historic symbol of reconciliation between Jews and Catholics. Instead it has become a source of recrimination. "If one uses terms like Warsaw Ghetto or racism in connection with Israeli or Palestinian politics, then one has forgotten everything, or learned nothing,"[200] the Israeli ambassador, Shimon Stein, said in a statement. The trouble had started back home in Germany when newspapers published more blunt remarks by two German bishops: Gregor Maria Hanke, of Eichstaett, and Walter Mixa, of Augsburg. "In the morning, we see the photos of the inhuman Warsaw Ghetto, and this evening we travel to the ghetto in Ramallah; that makes you angry," Bishop Hanke declared. Bishop Mixa described the situation in Ramallah as "ghetto-like" and said it was "almost racism." A third member of the delegation, Cardinal Joachim Meisner, the archbishop of Cologne, likened Israel's security barrier to the Berlin Wall. "I never thought I would have to see something like this ever again in my life," said Meisner, who is from the former East Germany. "This is something that is done to animals, not people." Despite reactions from Israel's ambassador to Germany, and from German Jewish leaders, the Catholic bishops were unrepentant. Neither Bishop Hanke nor Cardinal Meisner and Bishop Mixa offered any apology. Germany's top Catholic official, Cardinal Karl Lehmann, criticized the anti-Semitic comparisons, but he stopped far short of condemning the bishops' rants. The German cardinal wrote to the Yad Vashem that the "oppressive situation" in the West Bank, "in the shade of security fences and walls in Bethlehem," was "reflected in some harsh statements." Practically, the German cardinal endorsed the bishops' slander against the Jews.

When several members of the top body of the Catholic Church in Germany allow themselves, only several hours after visiting the

---

[199] "Aria di crociata" by Paolo Zanini, Edizioni Unicopli, 2012
[200] Haaretz, March 7, 2007

Yad Vashem Holocaust Museum, to associate the horrors of the Holocaust with the situation in the Territories, this gives rise to a question: to what extent is the Catholic Church still tainted by anti-Semitism? The outrageous and horrible comparison between Israeli efforts to prevent terror attacks and Nazi efforts to wipe out European Jewry is demonstrably false. The Warsaw Ghetto was created by the Nazis as a means of collecting Jews in preparation for their extermination by Zyklon B. How can a bishop compare it to an Arab city under the Palestinian Authority's rule?

In 2007, a group of Irish Catholic bishops called into question Ireland's commercial ties with Israel, saying Israel has made the Gaza Strip "little more than a large prison" for Palestinians. "Where there is evidence of systematic abuse of human rights on a large scale, as in the Occupied Territories, there are questions that must be asked concerning the appropriateness of maintaining close business, cultural and commercial links with Israel," said auxiliary Bishop of Dublin Raymond Field.

Archbishop James Vernon Weisgerber, the Catholic Church's leader in Canada, in January 2008 said to the Vatican Radio that "the Palestinians are treated less than humans."[201] Weisgerber is the head of the Catholic bishops in Canada and released that declaration after a visit in the disputed Territories. Another example is Robert Stern, who presides over the Pontifical Mission for Palestine, in an interview with the 30 Giorni magazine, directed by Giulio Andreotti, the Italian Senator and former prime minister, referred to the "Concentration camps for Palestinians."[202]

As noted earlier in this book, when eight Catholic bishops from Europe and North America visited Gaza in January, 2012, French Archbishop Michel Dubost drew a moral equivalency of sorts when he said that he had asked prisoners in the largest prison in Europe to pray for the Gazans; hence the symbolism was of one set of prisoners praying for the other. The Catholic Church news agency, www.news.va, published a report on the event, writing,

---

[201] Arutz Sheva, March 14, 2008
[202] "Campi di concentramento per i palestinesi," 30 Giorni, no. 5, 2006

"The signs of the 2009 conflict and the continuing Israeli air strikes are all around..." Not a word about the Islamic repression of that tiny Christian community in Gaza — and Bethlehem and the rest of the PA. The prison comparison was reiterated by another bishop. "I have just returned from visiting two of the largest 'open prisons' in the world – Bethlehem and the Gaza Strip," wrote William Kenney, auxiliary bishop in Birmingham who led the Catholic delegation. Bishop Patrick Kelly said that "violence is evil especially when it blocks humanitarian relief desperately needed."

A few days before, Palestinian Hamas leader, Mahmoud al Zahar, met with Father Manuel Musalam, head of the Catholic community in Gaza, known for having a radical anti-Jewish stance (in 2006 Musalam met also with Khader Habib, a senior Islamic Jihad official in the Gaza Strip). "Christians are not threatened by Muslims" – Musalam said – everyone faces the same problem, that of Israel's "humiliation."

In 2010 a senior Catholic bishop in Poland claimed Jews have stolen the Holocaust and exploited it to gain "unjustified advantages." The Shoah is a "Jewish invention."[203] Bishop Tadeusz Pieronek's remarks were published only hours before Israeli Prime Minister Benjamin Netanyahu arrived in Poland to take part in commemorations to mark the 65th anniversary of the liberation of the Auschwitz death camp. Pieronek, a personal friend of John Paul II and a former head of Polish bishops, went on to suggest that Jewish manipulation of the Holocaust had helped to silence international criticism of Israel's treatment of the Palestinians. He said: "When we see pictures of the wall (in the West Bank), we can see the colossal injustices committed against the Palestinians, who are treated like animals and have their rights violated, but, in the international lobbies, little is said. Let us establish an international memorial day for them. But they, the Jews, have a good press, because of their powerful financial

---

[203] Ynetnews, January 25, 2010

resources – extremely powerful through the unconditional support of the United States. And this promotes a kind of arrogance, which I consider to be unbearable."

During the 2009 war in Gaza, Cardinal Renato Martino, the head of the Vatican Council for Justice and Peace and a former Holy See envoy to the United Nations, compared Gaza to a "concentration camp."[204] On the sixtieth anniversary of the liberation of Auschwitz, public opinion moved suddenly and savagely from blaming the Jews for brutalizing Palestinian children to the memory of the victims of the Holocaust and the lessons to be learned from it. This is a dangerous and dreadful association. The Vatican "concentration camp" claim is a blatant anti-Semitic lie and an insult to the millions who really did suffer and die in the camps, and the Pope should have denounced it and chastened the cardinal who promoted it. Instead Martino confirmed the message to the press and the Vatican remained silent. The list of Vatican officials who Nazified Israel is much longer, but this overview should give us an idea of how deep is the perversion of the Shoah in the most influential Catholic quarters. When the declaration Nostra Aetate — literally In Our Age, the declaration on the relationship of the Church with Non-Christian religions — was published in 1965 within the framework of the Second Vatican Council, Catholic and Jewish scholars alike praised the step apparently taken by the Church in reducing the Church's anti-Semitism. This declaration remains the only theological step forward toward Jews since the Gospels. But at the same time as this step was being made, an attempt was underway to Christianize, relativize and trivialize the Holocaust. The extermination of the six million was recruited as a political weapon against Israel. That is why during the 2009 Gaza war, the American writer Cynthia Ozick proposed to abolish the memorial days in Europe, as the West is perverting the Shoah.

---

[204] The New York Times, January 8, 2009

Pope John Paul II began to transform the Holocaust into a Catholic event while he was a Cardinal in Poland, Karol Wojtyla. In 1970, at the ceremony for the beatification of Maximilien Kolbe in Rome, he distributed ashes from Auschwitz to the bishops present. Was he aware of the affront to Jews which would result from the touching, removing, and distributing of the remains of Jews' dead bodies — actions considered by Judaism as a desecration of the dead? "The Church of Poland," said Wojtyla, "since the beginning of the post-war period, sees the necessity of such a site of sacrifice, of an altar and a sanctuary, precisely in Auschwitz." The beatification of Kolbe was the first stone of a gigantic design: the "Christianization of the Shoah."[205]

Speaking in Auschwitz on 7 June 1979 – in the so called "Homily of Birkenau" – the Pope said that "there are six million Poles who lost their lives during the Second World War: one fifth of the nation." He did not mention Jews. In the homily, he called Auschwitz "the Golgotha of the contemporary world."[206] That is the hill in Jerusalem on which Jesus was killed, the most central site in Christianity. John Paul II went on to support the erection of a convent in Auschwitz. Later, under pressure from public opinion, he accepted that the convent be moved a distance of 500 meters away. Golgotha has been an expression often used by the Vatican to describe the Palestinians under the Israeli "oppression." The towering wooden cross in the Carmelite Convent grounds overlooking Auschwitz opened old wounds. If Auschwitz becomes the new Golgotha, then an Israeli checkpoint is easily turned into the site of a new crucifixion.

On July 14 1989, US Rabbi Avraham Weiss scaled a 7-foot fence at Auschwitz.[207] He and six students made their way to the entrance of the convent. Wearing Jewish yarmulkes and prayer shawls, the group loudly protested the presence of the convent and

[205] "The kidnapping of the Holocaust," Jerusalem Post, August 25, 1989
[206] "Constantine's Sword" by James Carroll, Houghton Mifflin (2001)
[207] "Memory Offended: The Auschwitz Convent Controversy," Carol Rittner (editor), Praeger, 1991

a 24-foot cross the nuns had erected over the pit of the dead. The group was prepared to settle in to spend the Sabbath outside the convent when a window opened and a Polish construction worker leaned out, holding a large kettle. He overturned the pot, dousing Weiss with paint. The Polish workers then began beating and kicking Weiss and his students. "That moment, when we were dragged and punched and kicked, was completely humiliating," said Weiss. "For a rabbi, for Jews, to be treated this way on the grounds of Auschwitz while the nuns looked on — it was symbolic of all that had happened there, and of the silence of the church during the Holocaust."

A group of 50 "Mengele twins" and their relatives also demonstrated outside the Carmelite convent. They vociferously demanded the removal of the Christian site from the camp and held up posters to that effect.

Poland's Catholic primate, Cardinal Jozef Glemp, warned the Jews against using their "powerful access to the media" to evict the nuns from Auschwitz and advised the Jews that they "should not look on Poles with a superior air and pose untenable positions." The homily was delivered before 150,000 Poles and the international media. Meanwhile, the Mother Superior of the Carmelite Sisters of Auschwitz, known as "Mother Teresa," gave an interview to the Polish-American weekly The Post Eagle, which editorialized in favor of the nuns' remaining at Auschwitz. Here are some of the highlights of the interview. The famous nun asked: "Why do the Jews want special treatment in Auschwitz only for themselves? Do they still consider themselves the chosen people?" She denies that there was any Polish "anti-Semitism" before World War II, pointing to the "fact" that "the Jews were an insignificant minority group in Poland with a majority of privileges." She accuses Israel of anti-Semitism for "mistreating the Arabs." As she put it: "Greater anti-Semites are hard to find," than the Israelis.[208]

---

[208] "A pious anti-Semite," The Jerusalem Post, November 14, 1989

It was one of the first expressions of the abuse of the Shoah used against Israel.

After visiting the concentration camp of Mauthausen on June 25, 1988, John Paul II said that the Jews "enriched the world by their suffering," and their death was like the grain which must fall into the earth in order to bear fruit, in the words of Jesus who brings salvation. One wonders whether being killed is the only role of the Jews in the eyes of the Pope. During the visit to Auschwitz, the Pope spoke of the Holocaust in these terms: "Six million Poles lost their lives during the Second World War — a fifth of the nation." We must remember as Cardinal Franciscek Macharski later said, that a previous papal sermon at Auschwitz inspired the Carmelite nuns, in autumn 1984, to create a convent where the Zyklon-B gas was stored to be used in the gas chambers.

Another step towards "Christianizing" the Holocaust has been the beatification of Edith Stein. "In the extermination camp she died as a daughter of Israel for 'the glorification of the holy name of God' and, at the same time, as Sister Teresa Benedetta of the Cross." According to the Vatican, in Edith Stein there is a fulfillment of "true" Judaism: the expiation of the guilt of being Jewish, the bridge transforming Auschwitz into Golgotha and preparing conversion of the Jews. Stein was born into an Orthodox Jewish family in Breslau, Germany, in 1922 she converted to Catholicism, and a decade later entered monastic life as a Carmelite nun. In 1987, Pope John Paul II beatified "Sister Teresa Benedicta" — taken after St. Teresa of Avila, founder of the Carmelite order — officially making her "a martyr of the Church." The Vatican tried to transform Stein in a Christian martyr, while she was in fact one of the countless Jewish victims of the Nazi death machine. It is because Stein died as a result of her Jewishness that the Jews have objected to the Catholic beatification. But according to the Pope, Stein demonstrated that the very symbol of Jewish martyrdom, Auschwitz, was not a Jewish event, or the expression of anti-Semitism nurtured by two thousand years of Christian teaching of contempt, but a place of Christian suffering and redemption. Stein was murdered by the

Nazis because she was Jewish according to the Nuremburg racial laws, and not because she was a Catholic. What had she done to provoke the Nazis who murdered her, other than being born Jewish?

In 1987 John Cardinal O'Connor, then Archbishop of New York, visited Yad Vashem, Israel's Holocaust museum. The Cardinal proclaimed that "the Holocaust is an enormous gift that Judaism has given to the world."[209] Jewish leaders had hoped that the Cardinal, who emerged as a leading exponent of John Paul II's orthodox teaching in the United States, would have been able to help shape a new Vatican policy toward Israel. But in fact, O'Connor's visit was a disaster for the Jews and Israel. To a people and a nation built upon the ashes of humanity's greatest crime, the idea that 6 million murdered Jews is a "gift" crosses the line from insensitivity to barbaric insult. And though the cardinal later apologized for the horrible remarks, O'Connor reopened one of the deepest wounds ever inflicted upon the conscience of the world: the Vatican silence during the Holocaust.[210]

The O'Connor trip was troubled from the start. On the eve of the visit, the Vatican ordered the Cardinal to cancel appointments he had made to meet Israel's leaders in Jerusalem (the Church had no diplomatic channels with the Jewish State). Columnist George Will in the Washington Post condemned O'Connor's "theology of suffering" about the Shoah: "The cardinal should understand how offensive it sounds to persons who are outside that circle and who once were within the barbed wire of Auschwitz."

The Holocaust's perversion has been instrumental in creating the Vatican's discourse on Israel. The January 2011 edition of Civiltà Cattolica, whose proofs are approved by the Vatican Secretariat of State, opened with a long editorial on the Palestinian refugees.[211] Adopting the Arab propagandist word "Nakba," used

[209] The New York Times, January 3, 1987
[210] "Jewish-Catholic amity is in danger," Chicago tribune, January 28, 1987
[211] "La fondazione dello Stato di Israele e il problema dei profughi palestinesi," La Civiltà Cattolica, January 2011

by the Palestinians to mourn Israel's foundation in 1948, the Vatican magazine declared that these refugees are a consequence of "ethnic cleansing" committed by the Jewish State. The journal also supported anti-Israeli historian Ilan Pappe, and falsely proclaimed that "the Zionists were cleverly able to exploit the Western sense of guilt for the Shoah to lay the foundations of their own state." The Civiltà Cattolica issue was one of many signs that the Catholic Church had adopted the Arab violent rhetoric meant to destroy the Jewish State.

The Holocaust-Nakba dual policy was pivotal in the official visit Pope John Paul II paid in Israel in March 2000. There were two highlights of the visit: the visit to Yad Vashem, with a meeting with survivors from Pope's own town, and the prayer at the Western Wall. The Pope said at Yad Vashem: "Only a Godless ideology could plan and carry out the extermination of a whole people." Thus all the responsibility falls upon a "Godless ideology," unrelated to or even opposing the Church. Already in March 1998, the Holy See, in the document "We remember: a Reflection on the Shoah," falsely stated, "The Shoah was the work of a thoroughly modern neo-pagan regime. Its anti-Semitism had its roots outside of Christianity."

Politically, the Pope was there for the Palestinians. He visited the Deheishe camp near Bethlehem, endorsing the "inalienable right" of Palestinian Arab refugees to repossess the homes and villages that they had lost in 1948, an act which would dismember the modern state of Israel. The Vatican always presented the 1948 war as the source of an "injustice" committed by Israel when it pushed away the Palestinians. It is worth recalling that the war was started by the Palestinian Arab leadership and the Arab regimes with the express purpose of destroying the Jews of Palestine and annulling the UN resolution calling for the establishment of a Jewish state. What is now often overlooked is that the refugee problem was created not by an inexorable eruption of hostilities, but by an Arab war of annihilation against Israel. On a more practical level, the purpose of the demand for "return" is to accomplish the goal of the Palestinian covenant — the dismantling of Israel — without having to engage in a frontal war.

John Paul II exclaimed "Do not be afraid!" from a pulpit in Jesus' birthplace. It was a day full of political symbolism, including a papal kiss on a bowl of Palestinian soil and a Muslim muezzin's call to prayer that sounded in Bethlehem just as the Pope finished a homily before 10,000 Christian and Muslim worshipers in front of the Church of the Nativity. He made the point more strongly when he was with Palestinian leader Arafat, saying, "No one can ignore how much the Palestinian people have had to suffer in recent decades. Your torment is before the eyes of the world. And it has gone on too long."[212] Pictures of refugees with slogans like "Refugees since 1948 — let them return" adorned walls and shop entrances.

The Pope's visit to Palestinian-controlled territory began with an official welcome from Arafat, who greeted Pope John Paul as "an esteemed guest in holy Jerusalem, the eternal capital of Palestine." In the Deheishe camp the Pope deplored "the degrading conditions in which refugees often have to live; the continuation over long periods of situations that are barely tolerable in emergencies or for a brief time of transit; the fact that displaced persons are obliged to remain for years in settlement camps." A large banner read in Arabic: "The right of return is a holy right and not for negotiation."

Deheishe has been a routine appointment for many Vatican envoys in the region. In 2004 Archbishop of Milan, Dionigi Tettamanzi, visited the Palestinian camp.[213] One of the landmarks of the camp is the Ibdaa Cultural Center. Established in 1995, the center's main goal is to educate Palestinians about the 1948 Nakba (catastrophe), the term used by the Palestinians to describe the creation of the State of Israel. "The right of return is a holy issue," says Ziad Abbas, director of Ibdaa. "For me as a refugee I don't believe that one day I will accept any compromise on the right of

[212] The National Catholic Reporter, March 28, 2000
[213] Il Corriere della Sera, June 20, 2004

return, or any pressure." Dr. Sari Nusseibeh, president of al-Quds University in Jerusalem, is one of the most hated figures in the camp. A leaflet distributed in the camp by Fatah activists denounced Nusseibeh as a "traitor" and threatened to "liquidate" him.

Deheishe has also been a notable source for suicide bombers. A terrorist's father, Munir Ja'arah, described a bombing as a "heroic operation," and said the family supports his son's decision to launch such an attack. "My son is a hero and we are proud of what he did," said Ja'arah, who lives in the Dehaishe refugee camp near Bethlehem. He was speaking as scores of Palestinians arrived at his home to "congratulate" him on the "martyrdom" of his son, Ali. Neighbors said that as soon as the bomber's identity was announced many local residents took to the streets to express their joy. Ali Ja'arah, the suicide bomber who worked as a policeman in Bethlehem, was also a member of Fatah's armed wing, the Aksa Martyrs Brigades. A leaflet issued by the terror group said the attack was intended "to show the Zionist enemy that the separation fence would not bring them security." Ali Ja'arah's uncle, Jihad Ja'arah, was one of the group's leaders in the Bethlehem area. He was one 13 Palestinian gunmen who were deported by Israel after they were holed up inside the Church of the Nativity in 2002 for several weeks. Jihad, who has been living in Ireland since he was deported from Bethlehem, said that he, too, is proud of his nephew's action.

While meeting Yasser Arafat in Bethlehem, the Pope offered him fourteen sea shells representing the fourteen stations of the Way of the Cross and the Pope explained that this was a way to symbolize the Passion of the Palestinians. Again, as with the Holocaust, the Pope made the comparison between the suffering of the Palestinians and those endured by Jesus. In a WikiLeaks cable on the Israeli/Palestinian conflict, Pope John Paul II decried "the injustice of which the Palestinian people have been victims for more than 50 years."[214] He added that only a halt to the violence and "respect for others and their legitimate aspirations, the application of international law, the withdrawal from occupied territories and internationally guaranteed status for the most holy places in Jerusalem," can break the cycle of violence. The Pope wants to revoke more than 50 years of injustice to the Palestinian people. If we count back from 2002, we will end up in 1952, or before. That means the 1967-line, is not enough to please the Vatican. Israel must give up more land, just as Hamas demands. In fact both Tel Aviv and Haifa are branded by Muslims as parts of "Palestine." As Islam claims, 1948 was the year of disaster. The Popes agree, of course in secret, with the Nakba's policy. This cable confirms that the Vatican holds the same views as Islam in regard to Israel.

As it is demonstrated by the Civiltà Cattolica edition of January 2010, the Vatican condemns Israel for the displacement of hundreds of thousands of Palestinian refugees during the 1948 war – a war that was started by Arab leaders who exhorted Palestinians to leave their homes to make way for the destruction of Israel – while ignoring the 800,000 Jewish refugees who were driven out of Muslim-majority countries in the Middle East in the years after Israel obtained its independence.

On 8th of May 2009 Pope Benedict XVI arrived on an official visit to Jordan and between the 11th and 15th of May he visited Israel and the Palestinian Authority. The Vatican authorities avoid calling the "State of Israel" by its name; they prefer to use the empty denomination "Holy Land." Speaking at Ben-Gurion airport on his arrival, the Pope immediately raised the subject of the Shoah to assuage the sense of guilt, "I will have the opportunity to honor the memory of the six million Jewish victims of the Shoah. Anti-Semitism... is totally unacceptable... I plead to explore every possible avenue... so that both peoples may live in

---

[214] http://wikileaks.org/cable/2002/01/02VATICAN180.html

peace in a homeland of their own, within secure and internationally recognized borders."

The Holy See views the Arabs as "victims" and the Israelis as "oppressors." Islamist terrorism can be traced back to this basic cause, as Cardinal Renato Martino, Chairman of the Pontifical Council for Justice and Peace, said in an interview to the L'Osservatore Romano on 1 January 2009, "Many problems that are now attributed almost exclusively to cultural and religious differences have their origin in countless economic and social injustices. This is also true in the complex history of the Palestinian people. In the Gaza Strip, human dignity has been trampled on for decades." Not a word was mentioned about Israel's withdrawal from Gaza in summer 2005 or Hamas' forceful seizure of power there in June 2007.

The abuse of the Golgotha passion marked the Pope's trip in Israel. In March 2000, on arriving in Bethlehem, John Paul II stated, "No one can ignore how much the Palestinian people have had to suffer in recent decades." In the Pope's message only the Palestinians suffered. Terrorism did not exist in the papal rhetoric. In his call for a Palestinian homeland John Paul used the words "international law and the relevant United Nations resolutions." This was a clear reference to the many anti-Israel UN resolutions passed by a General Assembly in which political factors weighed against Israel. Some understood the call by the Pope to link the birth of Jesus with the events of today as an attempt to link the suffering of Jesus with that of the Palestinians. "This is a place that has known 'the yoke' and 'the rod' of oppression. How often has the cry of innocents been heard in these streets?" John Paul II asked.

It was clear from the next Pope's speeches in Bethlehem and its surroundings, that the Catholic attitude to the Jewish people remains unchanged. He acknowledged the suffering of the Palestinians, the families left homeless, and offered his solidarity to "the people who have suffered so much." Pope Benedict told President Mahmud Abbas, that "the Holy See supports the right of your people to a sovereign Palestinian homeland in the land of your forefathers, secure and at peace with its neighbors, within internationally guaranteed borders." After expressing clear support for the Palestinian state, the Pope added that "Palestinians like any other people, have a natural right to marry, to raise families, and to have access to work, education and health care," hinting that the Israelis are not allowing poor Palestinians to marry and to have access to work, education, and medical care. Rather, the contrary is true.

Pope Benedict did not condemn Palestinian terrorism but launched an appeal to young people: "Have the courage to resist any temptation you may feel to resort to acts of violence or terrorism."[215] His words "temptation for terrorism" again hinted at the Vatican's claim that Israeli violence provokes Arab terrorism, while the truth is exactly the opposite. Pope Benedict XVI's message at the village of Al–Aida, located near Bethlehem, was also meant to symbolize the Arab claim of the "right of return," according to Fouad Twal, Latin Patriarch of Jerusalem.[216] Benedict XVI attacked Israel's security wall saying that "it is tragic to see that even today walls are erected" and later added that "walls can be brought down" — a clear incitation to violence.

In Vatican policy, the Holocaust has become a counterweight to the recognition of the Jewish condition in politics and history, which is the recognition of Jews as a people at stake with Israel and Zionism. The Catholic recognition of the Holocaust (dead Jews) justifies the denial of the Jews as a sovereign subject of history (living Jews). When Benedict XVI came to Israel in 2009, all cameras and microphones were pointed at Yad Vashem to report on the "German pope" about to speak on the Holocaust. The anti-Semitic stance taken by the Vatican in Bethlehem was barely noticed.

Pope Benedict XVI proclaimed the "land of the ancestors" of the Palestinian people and the State of Israel as defined by the

---

[215] Reuters, May 13, 2009
[216] The Daily Telegraph, April 27, 2009

Holocaust and facing a real people, aboriginal and native, heir of ancient Israel. Why would the Pope visit a refugee camp if not to certify the Arab narrative?

In his speech in the Palestinian territories, the Pope said, "May He bless with peace, the Palestinian people!" At the Aida refugee camp, "May God bless his people with peace!" In his homily in Manger Square, "You, God's chosen people in Bethlehem." In his speech to Palestinian president Abbas, "I invoke upon all the Palestinian people the blessings and protection of your heavenly Father." Unfortunately, we didn't hear the same blessings on the people of Israel. Pope Benedict's words also contained an encouragement to violence. By praising the "right of return" of the refugees, the Pope was asking the disappearance of the State of Israel. The Pope expressed his "solidarity with all Palestinians who have no home and waiting to return to their homeland." This is the best way to uphold the Palestinians in their plan to eradicate the Jewish State.

How to find words of peace in the Pope's condemnation of the "wall"? Before leaving Mahmoud Abbas, the Pope became very combative: "I saw the wall that intrudes into your territories, separating neighbors and dividing families. Although walls can easily be built, we know they do not last forever." Has the Pope forgotten that before the barrier Palestinian terrorism was rampant in the Israeli cities? Why did the Pope define the failure to commit terrorist acts as "courageous," if not to assume implicit understanding for such a "temptation"? The Pope said to the Palestinians, "Have the courage to resist any temptation you may feel to resort to violence or terrorism." To condemn the blockade of Gaza, the Pope has shown the same selective memory about "the embargo to be lifted soon." Not a word about Hamas and the 14,000 rockets Israel received from that territory after it evacuated the Jewish settlers in 2005.

Moreover the Pope resorted to anti-Jewish theology when he said that "I have seen with anguish the situation of the refugees who like the Holy Family were obliged to leave their houses," which recalls the Gospel of Matthew (2,13): 'Get up, take the child and his mother and escape to Egypt... Stay there until I tell you, for Herod is going to search for the child to kill him.'" If the Israelis are like Herod, are the Palestinians the modern version of Jesus?

7. THE ANTI-SEMITIC WITCHCRAFT

From Damascus to Durban

The industrial mass murder of Jews was not on the list of priorities of Pope Pius XII, the reigning pontiff during the Holocaust. The same could be said of Josef Stalin, F.D. Roosevelt and Winston Churchill, but they did not claim to be the "Vicar of Christ" on earth. The apologists exonerate Pius XII by saying that he did not understand the Holocaust. They are wrong. The Pope knew about the Shoah.

Pius was given daily briefings of Nazi atrocities by the British envoy to the Holy See. The pontiff resisted calls from Roosevelt's representative to the Holy See, the president of the Polish government in exile, the bishop of Berlin, and the chief rabbis of Palestine to speak out forcefully on behalf of the Jews. The Pope could have done much to stop the Zyklon B gas. He did little or nothing.

Historian Raul Hilberg wrote in his magisterial work "The Destruction of the European Jews," that for the Nazis, the rescue of thousands of Jews "was not nearly as important as a fact which was to have tremendous significance... not only then, but in years to come: the silence of the Pope." How many Catholic SS men and Nazi functionaries would have failed, at the very least, to have had second thoughts about their work had the Pope, for example, ordered Vatican Radio to broadcast round-the-clock denunciation of the Shoah, condemning it ex cathedra, and excommunicating the perpetrators? And how many Jews hearing such broadcasts from the voice of the Vatican would have learned that Jews' "resettlement" was a euphemism for death by gas?

In a landmark 1950 article for Commentary, historian Leon Poliakov wrote, "It is painful to have to state that at the time when gas chambers and crematoria were operating day and night, the high spiritual authority did not find it necessary to make a clear and solemn protest that would have echoed through the world."

During the Holocaust, most Christian Churches stood by in silence, or collaborated, when Jews were taken away by other Christians to be tortured and burned in Auschwitz. This Christian silence justified the murder of Christianity's brothers by the Christian authority. The Catholic Church and the relief organizations were suffering from the moral blindness induced by centuries of Christian "teaching of contempt," in which the Jews were demonized as "deicides," "moral lepers," and "agents of the devil" for their refusal to accept Christianity. That is why Pius XII did intervene only on behalf of baptized Jews, since they were considered by the Church as Catholics. The Pope chose cowardice in the face of evil. That is why our moral judgment of the Catholic Church about the most important modern event concerning Jews should remain that of culpability. While millions were devoured in the crematoria and Jewish skin was used for lampshades, the Pope turned a blind eye to the Israelite cataclysm. Et Papa tacet.

The Vatican's silence in the face of anti-Semitism surfaced again sixty years later during a papal journey in Syria. When the Pope travels, the world pays attention. That is why he makes his pilgrimages. They become his teaching moments. When John Paul II visited Syria in the summer of 2001, President Bashar el Assad greeted the Pope with a call for Christians to join forces with Muslims against Jews. Assad's display of pure anti-Semitism exploited the Pope's appeasing effort to honor the Arab world. But the question quickly shifted to the failure of John Paul II and the Vatican authorities, speaking then or later, to firmly repudiate the Arab-Muslim reiteration of the blood libel against the Jews.

Assad invoked the "agony of Jesus Christ" to equate it with the suffering of "the peoples of Lebanon, the Golan, and Palestine." Once again Jews are crucifying Christ in those peoples. Therefore, as Assad put it, "We expect Your Holiness to be on their (the people's) side." "There are those who always seek to repeat the agony march of all the people: we see our brothers in Palestine murdered and tortured, justice trampled and lands in Lebanon, the Golan and Palestine conquered in this way," Assad said to the Pope. "We hear them killing the principle of equality, saying that 'God has created our people separately from other peoples'; we see them mistreating the places sacred to Islam and Christianity in Palestine, violating the sanctity of the al-Aqsa Mosque, the Church of the Holy Sepulcher in Jerusalem, and the Church of the Nativity in Bethlehem. They are trying to kill all the values of the Monotheist religions, with the same mentality that brought about the betrayal and torturing of Christ and in the same way that they tried to betray the Prophet Muhammad..."

As James Carroll said, "Assad, in his anti-Jewish diatribe, gave John Paul II what could have been the most potent teaching moment of all." John Paul II could have said to the entire world that the definition of Jews as the enemy of God is lethal and racist; that Assad's attempt to recruit the Pope is nothing less than a holy war, not only against Israel, but against all Jews. The Pope could have labeled this Nazi incitement for what it was, firmly condemning it. Nothing. The Pope could have said that the Church has renounced the idea that Jews as a group can in any way be held responsible for the death of Jesus. Nothing. The Pope could have acknowledged that anti-Semitism is a consequence of ancient Christian slander. Nothing.[217]

The Syrian journey was a defining moment for Vatican failure to address the rejection of Israel in the Islamic world. In fact similar things were said by the Syrian president in interviews with European media during his visits to Paris and Berlin in June and July 2001, a few weeks after the Pope's visit. In an interview with the German Der Spiegel, Assad compared the suffering of Jesus to that of the Palestinians. When the interviewer observed that

---

[217] "A papal sin of silence," Jerusalem Post, May 13, 2001

mentioning Jesus' suffering implies that the Jews are to blame for it, Assad replied: "These are historical facts, which we cannot deny." The Pope's visit to Syria also took place during the Second Intifada, when Israeli buses, restaurants, schools, shopping malls and houses were bombed every day by suicide attacks, shootings and mortars. When Assad bragged that St. Paul set out from Syria to preach "the new religion" of Christianity, the Syrian explicitly contrasted it with the injustice of the old religion, Judaism. In response, the Pope could have insisted that Paul, too, remained a faithful Jew to the day he died, and that, indeed, he warned Gentiles against contempt for the God and people of Israel (Romans 9-11). The Pope could have made clear again that the church honors and affirms the biblical and historic Jewish connection to the Holy Land. But even a year before, the Pope should have firmly repudiated the increasingly circulated idea that traditional Jewish claims to the Temple Mount and Jerusalem have no basis in history. Tragically, this lie was at the root of Palestinian rejectionism.

The Pope travelled to Damascus to preach Mideast "toleration between different faiths." But he didn't refute the Christ-killer canard, and responded with general appeals for peace. A false peace. It is the same behavior of Pope Pius XII during the Holocaust. Joaquin Navarro-Valls, the Vatican spokesman, sniffed, "We couldn't care less" about Syrian efforts to manipulate the Pope's visit.[218] Navarro-Valls added: "The position of the Holy See regarding anti-Semitism is very clear." Not in the Middle East, it isn't. The Pope's lack of direct hard response to Assad's Nazism was taken by millions of people as an endorsement. If only the Pope had addressed the anti-Jewish canards directly, that, at least, would have created a moment of inspiration in a region that otherwise looks very dark. "It is one thing for the Vatican to repair relations with the Muslim world, as long as it is not done at the expense of the Jewish people,"[219] said Abraham Foxman, the

[218] The New York Times, May 7, 2001
[219] Jewish Telegraphic Agency, July 19, 2001

national director of the Anti-Defamation League. "It is nonsense for the Vatican to say we had nothing to do with this, because they provided a megaphone for this bigotry," Foxman continued.

Compounding the Pope's sin was the fact that it was his presence that provided Assad with the platform, and global television coverage, to preach his odious anti-Jewish venom. "I can understand the Pope's practices," said Seymour Reich, the chairman of the International Jewish Committee for Interreligious Consultations, an umbrella group of Jewish organizations. "But I am a little disappointed that there wasn't some sort of diplomatic way for the pope to indicate his annoyance and irritation – which he must have felt at Assad for taking advantage of his pilgrimage." The price of the Vatican's policy, Fisher conceded, "is that the pope can't respond when he disagrees at that moment. But he's perfectly free to go back to Rome and clarify what needs to be clarified. On the charges of Christ-killer, though, that is very clear and doesn't need to be clarified. It is one of the most solid building blocks of church teaching today and everyone knows it. Every other reading is misinterpretation."

L'Osservatore Romano, the Vatican official daily, didn't report on the words of the Great Mufti of Damascus, Ahmed Kaftaro, the highest religious authority in Syria who was with John Paul II when the Pope visited a mosque in Damascus. In the newspaper As Soura, the mufti wrote that the suicide bombers against Israel "represent the highest level of sacrifice and honor," that "the actions of the martyrs are the only tool against the Zionist military" and that Israel "is Nazi and racist." The Vatican should know that Syria's tightly controlled police state sponsored the publication of the infamous anti-Semitic czarist forgery, "The Protocols of the Elders of Zion." The Pope and the Vatican bureaucracy should have addressed this topic in public.

A few weeks before the travel to Damascus, John Paul II had visited the Babi Yar site, the Nazi shooting site during the Second World War. The Vatican might have been wise to denounce the international Holocaust-denial conference in Damascus by year's

Giulio Meotti

end. The conference — which tried to "scientifically prove" that the Holocaust never took place — was organized by French propagandist Roger Garaudy, a former Communist who converted to Islam, and his Iranian-based Swiss cohort, Jurgen Graf. Garaudy claimed Jews "invented" the Holocaust to justify the establishment of Israel.

Following close on Assad's remarks against the Jews to Pope John Paul II, Defense Minister Mustafa Tlas asserted that killing Jews is a duty for Arabs: "When I see a Jew before me, I kill him,"[220] Tlas said in an interview on Lebanese TV during the Pope's visit. "If every Arab did this, it would be the end of the Jews." In addition to the Tlas outburst, the official Syrian daily Tishrin accused Israel of a long list of massacres: "The contemporary Zionists are the same as those Jews who were fought by Jesus Christ."

Jewish criticism of Pope John Paul II mounted with Nobel Laureate Elie Wiesel saying the Vatican's failure to condemn the anti-Jewish blood libel by Syria's president has triggered one of the worst Catholic-Jewish crises in a generation. At no point during the four-day visit did the Pope or the Vatican condemn the Syrian attacks on the Jewish people. The Vatican envoys had no problems to meet Syrian Minister of Defense Tlass, whose book, "The Matzah of Zion," perpetuated the lie that Jews use Christian blood to bake Passover matzos. The Vatican had no time to spend some words about this anti-Jewish hatred in Syria, a nation that enabled a number of leading Nazi war criminals to find postwar political asylum.

In case Assad's twisted theological reflections were lost on his audience, Syrian Religious Affairs Minister Muhammad Ziyadah made sure the point was clear, noting: "We must be fully aware of what the enemies of God and malicious Zionism conspire to commit against Christianity and Islam." And what was the

[220] National Review, May 24, 2001

response of the pope, leader of hundreds of millions of Catholic faithful around the world, to this outrageous anti-Semitic outburst?

Silence. Nothing but silence. On his visit to Syria, the Pope was also the most recent in a long line of prominent guests ushered by the government to the demolished town of Quneitra, there to witness in the rubble of flattened buildings evidence of alleged "Israeli brutality."[221] Such visits, complete with former residents bussed in to lament their fate, have been regular fare since 1974, when Syria regained Quneitra under a UN-brokered agreement and immediately charged that Israel had maliciously destroyed the town with bulldozers and dynamite before the hand over. The Syrian and UN charges notwithstanding, the facts tell a different story.

Quneitra, in the Golan Heights, was captured by Israel in the 1967 Six Day War, suffering heavy damage. By the time Israeli troops entered the town, most of the population had fled. Between the 1967 war and the Yom Kippur War in 1973, Syria did not hesitate to shell Israeli forces stationed in Quneitra, further damaging the town. And during the 1973 war, Quneitra was repeatedly shelled by Arab (not just Syrian) artillery and tanks. The following year, as part of the disengagement agreement, Quneitra was handed back to Syria. Rather than repairing the damage and allowing Quneitra's residents to return as called for in the agreement, however, Syria has instead left the town in ruins and put up billboards and a museum to expose what it charges are "Zionist crimes."

The Pope's very presence in Quneitra provided a striking visual showcase for the Syrian government's efforts to portray the Church as its ally against Israel. Syrian television covered the visit live, frequently cutting away from the Pope to broadcast lingering close-ups of concrete rubble. The Pope's visit was meant to solicit Israel's withdrawal from the region, which would translate into another war of aggression against the Jews. The Vatican agreed to

---

[221] "Syria's Quneitra Hoax" by Alex Safian, Camera, May 10, 2001

play this game despite the fact that Golan Heights is a sovereign Israeli territory, home to 20,000 Jewish citizens, a national enterprise of dozens of communities with agriculture, wineries, a tourism industry, spas, and a history that dates back more than 3,000 years. Syria controlled the Golan for only 21 years, half the period it has been under Israeli rule. Why did the Pope agree to support the horrible "occupation" canard? Almost half of Golan's territory had been purchased by Rothschild and later robbed by the Syrian government. Jews settled in the Golan as early as 1886 but they were expelled, massacred, or fled because of malaria. The Golan is where the Jewish tribes of Dan and Menashe settled, and Israeli kings ranging from Saul to Herod ruled there. The Golan saw consecutive Jewish settlement for 800 years; 300 Jewish communities from the time of the Mishna and Talmud were discovered there, along with the remnants of 27 synagogues. Later, 1,000 years of desolation followed, until the Jews returned. The Golan belongs to the Jews because it is the estate of their forefathers and not only by the power of occupation in a defensive war against an aggressor, which is the case for the state of Texas in America and Poland and former German territories.

The Vatican knew that at the Arab summit held in Amman before the Papal visit, Assad had claimed that Israeli society is "more racist than the Nazis." The Vatican knew that the state-controlled Syrian media lambasted the Jewish State using vicious anti-Semitic imagery. In a report published on the portrayal of Jews and Israel in Syrian schoolbooks, the Center for Monitoring the Impact of Peace concluded, "The Jews are represented as evil, as a danger to the Arabs and to Islam, as a nuisance to humanity who have brought persecution and anti-Semitism upon themselves." A textbook used by Syrian tenth graders speaks of "the aggressive and evil disposition rooted in the Jewish personality the logic of true justice obligates one verdict on them from which there is no escape — that their criminal intentions be turned against them with their extermination."

As Yehudit Barsky, Middle East Affairs director of the American Jewish Committee, noted, it is "imponderable" that the

Pope would remain silent while a head of state like Assad would spew "falsehoods about Judaism in front of 1 billion Christians." For as the Church's relations with the Jews over the centuries amply demonstrate, even the most spurious of lies can ultimately have the most dangerous and lethal consequences. The Vatican knew that Syria was the place where in 1840, the most horrible blood libel against the Jews was proclaimed (see below). Centuries ago this blood libel was believed enough that many Jews were murdered on its account.

In 1991, the Syrian delegate to the UN Commission on Human Rights urged the commission to read the book "Matzah of Zion" in order to learn the "historical reality of Zionist racism." In 12th-century England, there were repeated stories of children being killed by the Jews for ritual purposes. As Hitler's minister of propaganda Joseph Goebbels so successfully taught, a lie, repeated often enough, will end up as truth, and the bigger the lie, the greater the likelihood that people will believe it. This is the case of a blood libel which was first leveled against the Jews in 1243 at Berlitz, near Berlin, and resulted in all of the town's Jews being burned. Over the centuries untold Jews were killed for their supposed heinous act of "killing the wafer."

On February 5, 1840 in Damascus, a Capuchin monk and his assistant vanished. The monks spread a rumor that, with the approach of the Passover, Jews murdered the Christians and siphoned off their blood to bake matzah. Catholic circles quickly alleged that the two had been kidnapped by the Jews to use their blood. The charge was supported by the French consul, Count Benoit Ratti-Menton. A barber named Negrin was brought to the French consulate, where he denied any knowledge of the missing men. Under torture, he "confessed" that Tomasso and his man were slaughtered by Jewish leaders, who were then tortured. Four of them died, but one, Moshe Aboulafia, could not stand the pain and "revealed" that he had left in his wife's custody a bottle filled with the friar's blood. After the wife denied any knowledge of the matter, the French consul beat her and took her to witness her husband being given two hundred lashes. Aboulafia, who was allowed to remain alive after converting to Islam, provided "quotes" from the Talmud to substantiate the blood libel accusations and accused prominent local Jewish personalities of being involved in the friar's death.

New persecutions occurred when bones were discovered in a dump in the Jewish quarter. Those were the remains of an animal, the Jews asserted, but Muslim and Christian "experts" swore they were human bones. The bones were interred, with great pomp, at the Capuchin monastery. The tombstone bore an inscription, in Italian and Arabic, attesting it was that of Tomasso of Sardinia who had been killed by the Jews. On the French consul's insistence, 60 Jewish children were arrested and kept in chains, in the hope they would accuse their parents of complicity in the ritual crimes. The blood libel charge was passed on to the Western press by the European consuls in Damascus, who took the details from their French colleagues without questioning the veracity of the absurd allegations. Even The Times of London, a most respected daily, printed the story without comment. One heroic exception is the great poet Heinrich Heine.

Born Jewish, Heine had converted to Christian Protestantism as a matter of convenience, but never stopped identifying with the people of Israel. A working journalist in addition to being Germany's most popular poet, he was one of the very few writers who interceded on behalf of the Damascus Jewish victims. Although Heine did not sign his articles in the Augsburg Allgemeine Zeitung, his articles on the blood libel affair were marked with a Star of David — a very clear indication of the writer's sympathies. Thus, what became known as "The Damascus Affair," passed into history as just one of many libels against the Jews which repeats itself — in a somewhat different guise — in today's world. However, this was not the Dark Ages, this was the enlightened modern world.

The year 2000 saw an explosion of such claims. Sheikh Nader Al-Tamimi, mufti of the Palestinian Liberation Army, told the Arabic language cable-news channel Al-Jazeera that there can be no peace with the Jews because they suck the blood of Arabs on Passover and Purim. The Pope in Syria could have used the visit to proclaim the evil of this witchcraft hard to die. He didn't. In November 1999 the government-controlled Syrian Arab Writers' Association published an article which mentioned the notorious story of the blood libel. At rallies around the world organized by Muslims protesting Israel's operation in Gaza, the chants of "baby killers" and "Israelis are Nazis!" were repeated again and again by the protestors. These sickening accusations have been picked up by Western media outlets and flashed on television all over the world. Time has come for Jews and non-Jews to respond to the haters of Israel and expose their blood libel to be as destructive and untruthful as the medieval accusations.

Today the Arab street is infested by hundreds of anti-Jewish plots. It is impossible to list them all. The latest is Yasser Arafat's assassination by the Israelis, exhumed along with rumors of how the villain met his death. There is the twisted lie accusing Israel of distributing drug-laced chewing gum and candy with the aim of killing children and sexually corrupting Arab women. There is the lingerie soaked with invisible ink for coded Jewish messages. In 2011 post-Mubarak Egypt scapegoated Israel for the E.Coli-infected farm exports that killed 48 Germans. The Arabs claim that powerful hormones are part of a Jewish plot to undermine Muslim piety and ensure Israel's domination over the Middle East. Other chemicals are used to turn the Arab daughters into nymphomaniacs and drive them into prostitution. Another favorite blood libel is that the Israelis are poisoning Arab water supplies. The rumors caused instances of hysteria, with dozens of Palestinian schoolgirls having to be hospitalized after fainting.

In 1982, the influential Syrian politician Mustafa Tlass published a best-selling book, *Matzah of Zion*, affirming the truth of the notorious 1840 case of blood libel in Damascus. Tlass's book has become influential in international anti-Semitic circles as a reliable source about Jewish ritual murder and has been published in multiple languages, including French and Italian. By 2002, Tlass's book was one of the most popular at the Syrian Book Fair.

According to its publisher, the reason for its popularity is "the will of the next generation to know about the Jews, how they harm Arabs and others." The Christian representatives in Syria and the Vatican delegation should have known about this long enmity against the Jews. In the 1920s, the Protocols of the Elders of Zion, the notorious anti-Semitic forgery, was firstly translated to Arabic from the French by Arab Christians. The first translation was published in Raqib Sahyun, a periodical of the Catholic Community of Jerusalem, in 1926. Another translation made by Arab Christians appeared in Cairo in 1927, this time as a book. The covers of both Tlass' editions show a man with his throat slashed and his blood collecting in a basin. The first edition's cover displayed a group of Jewish people carrying out the murder, sketched to look "Jewish" according to Nazi depictions. The second edition features a Menorah, the Jewish symbol, cutting throats.

Damascus has been the safest heaven for the architects of the Shoah and when the Pope visited Damascus high profile Nazi officers were living there. The most notorious was Alois Brunner. 45,000 Austrian Jews were deported under his command. He then deported to Auschwitz 46,000 Greek Jews. Other 26,000 Jews were deported from France. On 31 July 1944, when the Allies were at the gates, Brunner arrested 300 children and sent them to Auschwitz. None survived. In Slovakia he deported 13,500 Jews. In 1954 Brunner ran to Egypt, where he trained the Egyptians in interrogation techniques in which he had become a master. Then he fled to Damascus. His home address has been George Haddad Street 7, and his new name was Georg Fischer, a German businessman. He was said to be living at the Meridian Hotel in Damascus. In a 1987 telephone interview to the Chicago Sun Times, Brunner stated on the Jews: "All of them deserved to die because they were the devil's agents and human garbage. I have no regrets and would do it again."[222]

---

[222] "Nazi butcher in Syria haven," Chicago Sun Times, November 1, 1987

The pro-Nazi Syrian regime proclaimed hatred for the Jews in front of the Pope. But the Vatican stood silent. And here we return to Pius XII during the Holocaust. During the war the Pope always spoke, and wrote, in generic phrases, in allusions, with judgments marked by indirectness, naming no names and no country. That is why Pius' behavior during the war has a very deep resonance in our days: Did the Church learn that the road to the hell is paved with silence? Exactly as during Pius XII's time, there are just two possible reactions: being concerned and resisting or being complacent and collaborating.

In 1994 Pope John Paul II drew Jewish and Israeli outrage by conferring the papal knighthood on Kurt Waldheim, former UN's General Secretary, Austrian President but most important, a Nazi war criminal. The Order of Pius IX is one of five orders that the Pope may bestow. Waldheim was accused of complicity in the Holocaust, and the evidence was hard enough to satisfy the U.S. Justice Department to ban him. Waldheim was the "everyman" who, when asked, put his shoulder to the Nazi wheel. The Pope's audience with Waldheim represented a virtual papal pardon for the Austrian head of state. As such, it was an insult to the Holocaust victims.

The Vatican embassy in Vienna said Waldheim received the knighthood in recognition of his "efforts for peace" during his tenure as United Nations Secretary General from 1972 to 1980. The Vatican knew that it was under Waldheim's administration at the United Nations that the diplomatic offensive to make Israel the pariah of the nations had been powerfully launched. The anti-Semitic UN resolution 3379 ("Zionism is racism") was passed on November 10, 1975, at a time when Waldheim was Secretary General.[223] It was at this time that Yasser Arafat, following his direct complicity in a number of high profile terrorist acts, addressed the General Assembly wearing army fatigues and holster. The Vatican knew Waldheim's horrible reaction to Israel's

---

[223] "Waldheim's Last Chapter," New York Sun, June 18, 2007. See also "The U.N.'s Man in the middle," New York Times, September 13, 1981

daring rescue of Jewish hostages at the Entebbe airport in 1976, when he called it a "serious violation of the national sovereignty of a United Nations member state." Never mind that the state was headed by Idi Amin and Amin's soldiers were helping the terrorists guard the hostages.

Israeli actions in southern Lebanon to protect the Jewish civilians had consistently drawn Waldheim's rebukes, the Palestinian violence was always played down or unidentified under Waldheim's tenure and although he denounced Israel for attacking the Iraqi nuclear reactor, he did not criticize Iraq for attacking Iran. In 1980 Waldheim, in remarks that went well beyond previous statements, expressed support for a Palestinian state. The Secretary General spoke to about 95 people at the Waldorf-Astoria dinner. Following is the portion of his speech, as recorded by the Arab League, which has aroused Israeli criticism: "I think there can be no doubt that a Middle East settlement can be achieved only if we find a solution for the Palestinian issue. As long as the Palestinian issue has not been resolved, there can be no comprehensive settlement of the Middle East question. This means that foreign forces have to be withdrawn from the occupied territories, including East Jerusalem. It also means that the legitimate rights of the Palestinians have to be respected."

Waldheim was one of the first worldwide leaders who legitimized Arab terrorism against Israel. The Vatican played a special role in helping him to gain international and political legitimization. In 1987 Pope John Paul II welcomed Waldheim to the Vatican as an honored state visitor and praised him for a lifetime of activity on behalf of peace. He made no mention that Waldheim was implicated in Nazi atrocities. Several Western ambassadors, including those from the United States, Britain, Italy and West Germany, stayed away from the ceremony with Waldheim to express their disapproval. Outside the huge, cordoned-off ellipse of St. Peter's Square, Jewish demonstrators chanted and waved placards against Waldheim's visit. Amid the slogans were placards listing the names of Nazi death camps such as Auschwitz, Dachau and Treblinka, and a miniature gallows complete with noose. Blue-and-white police helicopters circled low over the demonstration, at times drowning out the protesters as they chanted "shame, shame" and "executioner, executioner," and sang Jewish songs such as Hatikvah, the Israeli anthem.

New York City Rabbi Avi Weiss and three other American Jewish activists wore concentration camp uniforms and Jewish prayer shawls. "The Vatican desecrates the souls of the 6-million Jews killed by the Nazis, so we will sanctify their souls by praying," Weiss said. Among the protesters also was German-born Nazi-hunter Beate Klarsfeld.[224] "We are here to show the Pope it was a big mistake to receive Waldheim," said Beate.[225] She also had a large placard reading, "Will Klaus Barbie be the Vatican's next guest?" Barbie is the former Gestapo chief of Lyon, France, whom Klarsfeld tracked down in Bolivia. "The Pope has condemned dictators such as (Polish leader Wojciech) Jaruzelski and (Chilean President Augusto) Pinochet. We had been minimally looking for an even stronger condemnation of Waldheim, whose hands are dripping with Jewish and Christian blood," Weiss said in a statement.

"We are more incensed than ever before by the Pope's praising of Waldheim's tenure as UN secretary general," Weiss said. "It was during Waldheim's period as secretary general that the United Nations equated Zionism with racism and that it welcomed Yasser Arafat, whose aim is to destroy Israel." The Israeli officials were also very critical of Waldheim's reception at the Vatican. Israeli Prime Minister Yitzhak Shamir described the visit as "an outrageous act," saying, "It could be interpreted as a justification for crimes of which Waldheim is accused."

Rabbi Mordechai Winyarz also wore the uniform of a concentration camp survivor to protest against the Pope's policy on Waldheim and Arafat. Why did the Pope meet with and praise Austrian President Kurt Waldheim, the former Nazi? Why was the Vatican silent during the Holocaust, when six million Jews

---

[224] "Rome police detain Waldheim protesters," San Francisco Chronicle, June 25, 1987
[225] "Protesters raise the specter of the Holocaust," Newsday, June 26, 1987

Giulio Meotti

perished? Why did the pope embrace the leader of the Palestine Liberation Organization, whose group is dedicated to the destruction of Israel? "Arafat's methodology is killing women and children. Waldheim is a documented Nazi," said Winyarz, whose mother survived the Holocaust. "What does that say when the Pope welcomes these men and embraces them?"[226]

In 2009 Pope Benedict XVI participated to an "interfaith" meeting at Notre Dame Hotel in Jerusalem. Sheik Tayseer Tamimi, the leading Palestinian Muslim cleric who heads the PA's Sharia courts, accused Israel of "murdering women and children and destroying mosques" and "destroying Palestinian cities." He also laid claim to Jerusalem as "the Palestinian people's capital," and called on those present to "defend the Palestinians against the expropriation of their lands."[227] In attendance were the Pope, the leading figures in the Rabbinate, Latin Patriarch Fuad Twal, and the heads of the Israeli branches of several churches.

Why did the Vatican accept hosting Tamimi? The Church knew that the Palestinian cleric was responsible for a similar incident in 2000, when Tamimi raged against the Jews during an interreligious dialogue in the same hall, attended by Pope John Paul II.[228] Tamimi welcomed the pontiff in Arabic as the guest of "the Palestinian people on the land of Palestine, in the city of holy Jerusalem, eternal capital of Palestine." He then said that he could not sit with rabbis as long as Palestine was occupied by Israelis. Tamimi spoke about Israel's "usurpation" and "aggression against people, property and holy places." John Paul II, who had an interpreter at his side, held his head in his hands throughout the anti-Semitic speech. The Vatican should have refused to participate to similar meetings with Tamimi. It would have sent a powerful message to the Muslim world.

In 1994, the Fatah-appointed Tamimi had stated, "The Jews are destined to be persecuted, humiliated, and tortured forever, and it

226 Miami Herald, September 10, 1987
227 The New York Times, May 11, 2009
228 The New York Times, March 24, 2000

is a Muslim duty to see to it that they reap their due. No petty arguments must be allowed to divide us. Where Hitler failed, we must succeed." Tamimi also called on Muslims to pray for the destruction of the United States. So why did Pope Benedict XVI wait until the end of Tamimi's speech to leave the hall? Why did no Vatican official respond to the Palestinian anti-Semitic attack? At the end, the cleric walked across the stage and shook Benedict's hand. The Pope did not react. The Anti-Defamation League rightly called on the Council of Religious Institutions of the Holy Land to expel the Muslim cleric who launched the hateful verbal attack against Israel.

The fact is that Tamimi was a well-known anti-Semite and Hamas supporter. He urged Palestinians and Christians to become homicide bombers against the Jews. Tamimi was sitting just a seat away from the Pope on-stage, that night. That didn't happen by accident, nor was it a surprise, despite what the Catholic organizers of that event claimed.[229] The Vatican never said they didn't invite Tamimi to sit onstage near the Pope. They only said he was not on the list of "scheduled speakers." And that is disgusting enough. They knew what Tamimi was about. It was not a secret. Yet, they didn't object to his presence onstage with the Pontiff.

The Vatican's inability to prevent Tamimi's disaster showed again the Church's moral indifference to the slander of Jews. Hundreds of members of nongovernmental organizations had gathered in the Notre Dame Cultural Center to hear an inspiring message from the Pope. Other Muslim religious leaders could have been invited who could have shown a more tolerant, open, respectful and dialogical approach to the Pope and the audience of hundreds of leaders and activists in interreligious dialogue.

The analyst of Middle East affairs, Barry Rubin, rightly wrote that "It is a pity that the Palestinian Authority's chief Islamic judge Tayseer Rajab Tamimi will be criticized for rudeness rather than incitement to genocide. And the whole political context of

---

[229] "Vatican, Organizers Lying About 'Unexpected' Taysir Tamimi Appearance" by Debbie Schlussel, May 11, 2009

Tamimi's statements shouldn't be missed either: he is an appointee of the PA." Tamimi's goal is to commit mass murder and make all Israeli Jews refugees. Tamimi's most notable appearance in history was when, as chief Islamic judge in Hebron, he was deported by Israel temporarily in 1980, the day after terrorists killed six Jewish theological students in that Jewish holy city.

Vatican forums provided publicity many times for anti-Zionist platforms. Another example of the so called "interfaith dialogue" used to demonize the Jews was the 2001 two-day conference of Muslim and Vatican leaders organized by the Sant'Egidio Community, a Catholic lay group with a history of mediating international conflicts, and that has many Vatican ties.[230] No Jews were invited to the meeting. The first speaker, Yusuf al Qaradawi, the Muslim Brotherhood guru, denounced Israel in this way: "We Arabs are among the most sensitive to this because of the evil inflicted on us by arrogant Zionists. We go to sleep at night and get up in the morning in a Palestine transformed into a continuous funeral. We refuse terrorism but don't consider it terrorism to defend one's own home." A few months later, Qaradawi was the main speaker of another meeting organized by the Vatican commission for the dialogue with Islam. It took place in Doha, Qatar, and along with Qaradawi as speaker, was Archbishop Michael L. Fitzgerald, president of the Vatican commission for interfaith dialogue, and the former Vatican foreign minister, cardinal Jean-Louis Tauran. Qaradawi issued fatwas calling for jihad against Israel and the Jews, and authorizing suicide bombing attacks even if the victims were women and children. He has also issued fatwas authorizing attacks on Jews around the world.[231]

After Qaradawi, came Cardinal Carlo Maria Martini, Archbishop of Milan, who many Catholics wanted to see elected as Pope. By the end of the morning, several other speakers had explicitly tied terrorism to the Israeli treatment of Palestinians, expressed strong anti-American feelings and shown how hard it

---

[230] Chiesa Espresso, March 22, 2002
[231] "Harsh words at Christian-Muslim meeting," New York Times, October 5, 2001

was even for some relatively moderate religious leaders to moderate their language when it came to recent events. Cardinal Martini and Cardinal Etchegaray listened to the anti-Jewish tirade without protesting. No protest came from the Vatican either.

And how to forget the meeting that Pope John Paul II had with the Sudanese Islamist Hassan al Turabi? The meeting took place in the Vatican on 13th of October, 1993. The Pope and his collaborators knew that Turabi was the most important exponent of Islamic anti-Semitism. The Pope knew that Turabi played a role in the execution of Mohammed Taha, whose "guilt" was of advancing of a dialogue between Islam and Judaism. The Pope knew that Turabi, two years before the meeting in St. Peter, had legitimize the policies of Saddam Hussein at a time when Iraq threatened to "burn half of Israel" with sarin gas and other chemical poisons. The Pope knew that Turabi at that time was sheltering in his Sudanese realm, Carlos the Jackal, the person mainly responsible for terror attacks against Jewish targets in Europe. The other famous guest of Turabi was a Saudi man named Osama Bin Laden.

In 1998 Pope John Paul II's visit to Austria included a meeting with the Vienna-based diplomatic corps, whose members include Robert Prantner, envoy extraordinary and minister plenipotentiary of the Knights of Malta. In a December 5 article in the Austrian publication Zur Zeit, Prantner argued that rather than the Catholic Church apologizing to the Jews for centuries of anti-Semitism, the Jews should apologize for "their deplorable crimes... against Catholic children like the holy martyr-child Anderl von Rinn, against adults in the days before Easter... and for the blood of murdered Christians, spilled by Jewish hands, which cries to heaven, too." Efraim Zuroff, head of the Simon Wiesenthal Center's Israel office, said "this theologian, Prantner, is basically saying that the blood libel is true — we're in 1998 for God's sake! This is outrageous. This is taking us back to the Middle Ages." The Knights of Malta is a Catholic lay order. While Prantner is not a diplomat, he is an employee of the Vatican. The blood libel accusing Jews of the ritual murder of Anderl von Rinn took place in the 17th century and was used to incite pogroms against the Jews. Responding to an incident involving a security check on the archbishop of Jerusalem by "Jewish officials" at Ben-Gurion Airport, Prantner compared the hatred of the "Jewish masters from Palestine" with "the clamor of the high priests of the Sanhedrim two millennia ago to crucify Jesus."

In 2009 Israeli Prime Minister, Benjamin Netanyahu, appealed to Pope Benedict XVI "to make his voice heard" and use his moral authority to condemn the harsh anti-Jewish rhetoric voiced by Teheran. The Iranian leader Mahmoud Ahmadinejad repeatedly called for Israel's destruction and questioned whether the Holocaust, in which 6 million Jews were killed by the Nazis, took place. "I asked him, as a moral figure, to make his voice heard loud and continuously against the declarations coming from Iran of their intention to destroy Israel," said Netanyahu. "I told him it cannot be that at the beginning of the XXI century there is a state which says it is going to destroy the Jewish state, there is no aggressive voice being heard condemning this," Netanyahu went on to say. Unfortunately, a few weeks later the Vatican stood silent in front of Iran's genocidal leader. In addition, Pope Benedict's decision to send a Vatican delegation to a United Nations conference on racism has opened a new rift in relations with Israel. The United States and some of its allies, including Italy a country which often sees eye-to-eye with the Vatican at international conferences — boycotted the meeting. Instead the Pope called the conference an important initiative and said he hoped it could help "put an end to every form of racism, discrimination and intolerance."

Chief Vatican spokesman, Father Federico Lombardi, defended the Vatican's presence and said a disputed conference text was "acceptable" because objectionable parts had been deleted.

Israel recalled its ambassador to Switzerland in protest before Iran's Ahmadinejad spoke. Abraham Foxman, director of the U.S.-based Anti-Defamation League, said the Vatican should have boycotted the talks after it learned that Ahmadinejad would attend.

"By participating, the Vatican has given its endorsement to what is being prepared there (against Israel)," Rome's chief rabbi Riccardo Di Segni said.[232]

Shimon Samuels, head of the European office of the Simon Wiesenthal Centre, said the Vatican "is giving a seal of approval in the hate campaign" against Israel. "This is not a position on which one can hedge," Samuels said. "You can't have it both ways. The Vatican is a powerful voice and (a boycott) could have had a strong demonstrative effect." The American Gathering of Holocaust Survivors and their Descendants expressed its "deep disappointment" that the Vatican did not join the boycott. "Because the conference highlights the participation of Iran's notorious Holocaust-denier Ahmadinejad there was a particular obligation for the Vatican to have stayed away," said the group's vice president, Elan Steinberg.

Who was host of the Durban II anti-racism conference? Libya, one of the world's worst perpetrators of racism, discrimination, and human rights abuses. Who was chosen to give the opening address? None other than Iran's Ahmadinejad. The same Ahmadinejad who openly says the Final Solution to peace in the Middle East is to wipe Israel off the map. The same Ahmadinejad who pays terrorist groups Hamas and Hezbollah to strap bombs to Arab women and children so they can blow up Israeli women and children. The same Ahmadinejad who believes it is his duty to speed the return of the Islamic savior, the 12th imam, by igniting World War III. Since October 25, 2005, when Tehran hosted an anti-Zionism conference, Iran's president called for Israel to "be wiped off the face of the map," the first in a long series of incendiary speeches advocating the liquidation of the Jewish State. Ahmadinejad then publicly warned Israeli Jews that their country "will one day vanish," "will be gone, definitely," and that "they are nearing the last days of their lives."

---

232 Reuters, April 20, 2009

The Iranian leaders are saying that the Israelis "are like cattle, nay, more misguided." They call the Jews "a bunch of bloodthirsty barbarians," "an insult to human dignity," a "stinking corpse," a "wild beast," and a "scarecrow." Like the Nazi weekly Der Stürmer portraying Jews as "parasites," and "locusts," or the Hutu propaganda in Rwanda against the Tutsis described them as "cockroaches," the Iranian leaders have called Israeli Jews "filthy," and "bacteria." Yahya Rahim Safavi, one of the founders of the Islamic Revolutionary Guards Corps and now senior adviser to Supreme Leader Khamenei, called Israel "impure," "unhygienic," and "contaminated."

The Vatican delegation didn't walk out. They just sat there. They listened to Ahmadinejad's anti-Jewish rant and stayed in place as the remaining pro Islamic delegates erupted in applause. The permanent envoy of the Vatican at the UN Human Rights Council, Silvano Tommasi, declared that "the point of Ahmadinejad's speech was the racism of the State of Israel against the Palestinians, but he didn't attack the Holocaust nor he mentioned the destruction of Israel. For this reason we, together with other European countries and the totality of African, Asian and Latin American nations decided to remain in the hall. To affirm the right to freedom of expression."[233]

It was as if Pope Pius XII had returned to silently watch the crowds jeering as the Nazis fed the Jews to the lions. Pope Pius XII earned the title "Hitler's pope" for his refusal to speak out against Nazi anti-Semitism and the mass extermination of Jews across Europe. But this isn't 1940. Today, Pope Benedict XVI reigns, Israel is a reality and people imagine the Vatican to have repented of its World War II shortcomings, its post-World war II ratlines that smuggled Nazis out of Europe, the Inquisition, and several hundred years' worth of Crusades. Then why is it that the number-one religion in the world didn't feel it had a moral responsibility to speak out against incitement to another Jewish

---

[233] La Repubblica, April 20, 2009

genocide? Why didn't it do anything besides just sit there and take it all in? Why did abandon Israel again?

If there is still any question as to whether or not Durban II had in fact a racist, anti-American agenda, all the proof you would ever need is Durban I. The whole purpose of Durban II was to reaffirm and ratify the findings of Durban I—the original UN-sponsored America-bashing hate-fest that singled out Israel alone, out of literally all countries in the world, as the example of a racist state.

The 2001 decision by the United States and Israel to withdraw from the first anti-Semitic conference of Durban over a working document that equated Zionism with racism drew criticism from the Vatican and a coalition of Catholic nongovernmental organizations. Well-known NGOs such as Amnesty International and Save the Children attached their names to the conference. Israel was declared an "apartheid" and "criminal" state, and the Jews, inveterate racists. NGOs at the conference supported the request of the Tanzanian minister of foreign affairs, Jakaya Kikwete, for immediate cash compensation to Africa for Western slavery. This fabricated colonial sense of guilt has become jet fuel for a corrupted humanitarian agenda.

Encouraged by these NGOs, the genocidal Zimbabwean dictator Robert Mugabe proclaimed that the Jews were responsible for all the ills of Africa. The mass of NGOs in the streets at the conference exalted Osama bin Laden, while the images of George Bush and Ariel Sharon were ornamented with swastikas and motifs of blood and death. Some NGOs distributed leaflets with a portrait of Hitler and the inscription: "What if Hitler had won? There would be no Israel, and no Palestinian bloodshed."

Again, the Vatican saw no reason to withdraw its delegation from this horrendous conference against the Jews. Archbishop Diarmuid Martin, head of the Vatican delegation and permanent observer of the Vatican to U.N. offices in Geneva, said the United States, which had withdrawn from the conference, could have made a positive contribution to the event. "I personally feel very sorry that a country, a nation which has had a unique experience in the fight against racism, something quite constructive from which we could all learn, and an ongoing experience, that it didn't feel it could serenely take part in the conference and bring up a positive contribution," Martin said.

Cardinal Wilfrid F. Napier of Durban said that in healing the sin of racism, an honest and sincere dialogue was necessary. "We're discussing racism, we're discussing poverty, we're discussing the issues, but we're not reaching across to solve them," Napier said of the U.N. conference. "I don't know how much is achieved by pointing accusing fingers," he said. Franciscan Sr. Bernadette Sullivan of the New York-based Franciscans International said the U.S. pullout was "very sad." "Walking out this way only hurts the United States. One more time they lose credibility with the world community," said Sullivan, a delegate to the U.N. conference. No, it is the Vatican which is losing credibility.

8. A SAFER WORLD FOR THE JEWS?

In the spring of 2011, 17 Jewish skeletons were found at the bottom of a medieval well in Norwich, England. The Jews were murdered or had been forced to commit suicide. The bodies date back to the 12th or 13th Centuries, at a time when Jewish people faced murder and banishment throughout Christian Europe. Those 17 Jews were killed because of "replacement theology," the most ancient Catholic calumny that says that because of their denial of the divinity of Christ, the Jews have forfeited God's promises to them, which have been transferred to the Church. "You are born after your father, the Devil," the Vatican proclaimed of the Jews during those pogroms. Ten centuries later, this theological demonology is directed against the heirs of the 17 Jews: the Jews of the State of Israel.

The excavations in England suggest the Jews were thrown down the well together, head first. The kids after the parents. Five of them had a DNA sequence suggesting they were likely to be members of a single Jewish family. In the same days of the excavations in Norwich, five Jews from the same Israeli family, the Fogels, were slaughtered in their own beds by Palestinian terrorists in the Samarian town of Itamar. A famous Italian Catholic priest, Mario Cornioli, wrote immediately after the massacre in a subliminal justification of the killings, "What is Itamar? An illegal Israeli colony built on stolen land." The replacement calumny has changed language, but it is still a death sentence for the Jewish people. Israelis, like Lucifer, were God's elect but were cast out for their rebellious and evil ways; so they now deserve to be obliterated from the so called "Holy Land."

The Dutch writer Leon de Winter said it very well: "Anti-Semitism Is Salonfähig Again."[234] It is a German word meaning socially acceptable. On March 2011 the Fogels were annihilated in Itamar. Father, mother and three children butchered during a night of horror which resembled the slaughter of the Clutter family in Kansas in 1959 (the event which inspired Truman Capote's masterpiece, *In Cold Blood*). It was a pogrom, like during the time of the Cossacks. In the city of Berdychiv, on January 4, 1919, militants stopped children who were studying the Torah, asking, "Jew?" If they said yes, they then shot them in the forehead. To those who offered money, they said, "We want your life!"

That night in Itamar a 12 year-old Israeli girl, Tamar, took part with other friends in a scouting event until midnight, close to her village, where 100 families live. She arrived home and knocked on the door. Nobody answered. She went inside with a neighbor and she saw her mother, her father, her three brothers (respectively 11, 3 years and 3 months old) slaughtered with their throats cut.

The Vatican, which professes to deplore violence on both sides of the Israel-Palestinian equation, has been totally silent on the slaughtering. Neither have words of condemnation about the deaths of these innocents at the hands of terrorists been heard from the usual human rights groups. The daily diet of hateful propaganda has had its intended effect. Itamar meant that no rational argument can be used against an ideology maniacally dedicated to Jewish destruction, and that says so in every language, at every opportunity. The dark and glittering eyes of Itamar's Arab terrorists are telling their desires of turning the Mediterranean Sea red with Jewish blood and erecting a "Palestine" on the ruins of Israel. It is the complacency of the West and the Vatican's silence in the face of a new killing spree of Jews.

---

[234] The Wall Street Journal, June 14, 2010

In recent years we have seen plenty of saccharine movies about Jewish children killed in the concentration camps in their pajamas, but the same public opinion reacted with indifference to the images of Israeli babies dismembered by terrorists one year ago. The Fogels, right down to the decapitated baby, were less human than other victims and therefore less deserving of Western outrage on their behalf. The "settler kids" in Adora, Elon Moreh, and Tekoa have become invisible, as the Galilean towns were during the '70s, when Yasser Arafat's terrorists murdered Jewish babies in Ma'alot, Kiryat Shmona and Avivim, and the Vatican, also at that time, stood silent, while Catholic commentators invited Israel of follow the Gospels instead the Talmud.

The Vatican's excuse for not speaking out against the crime in Itamar might be because the "anger" of the perpetrators is justified in international eyes. PA's President Mahmoud Abbas said many times that "I will never allow a single Israeli to live among us on Palestinian land." Such a state, supported by the Vatican diplomacy and advocated officially by many Popes, would be the first to officially prohibit Jews or any other faith since Nazi Germany, which sought a country that was "jüdenrein," or cleansed of Jews. That a nationalist Arab movement which supported Hitler should call the presence of Jews an obstacle to peace is one thing. It is quite another for an "enlightened world," or the Vicar of Christ, to do so. But this is the precise reason why Itamar didn't cause any global scandal. And it is the precise reason the Vatican didn't raise its voice to protest against the beheading of Jewish babies in their homes.

In a world less surreal than the one we live in, the act of bursting into a Jewish home and slitting the throats of Jewish babies would be the cause of moral and religious outrage. Multiply this act by thousands and one might think it would rate an international uproar. Yet in the world in which we live, Itamar was a marginal note at the end of the page. It didn't get even a note of disgust from the Vatican. Neither the US institutionalized Churches nor the Vatican made reference to

Itamar's attack at all. Nor did the UNICEF (United Nations Children Fund) raise its voice against the genocidal destruction of innocent Jewish babies. The mainstream media contained years of fabricated justification: because Itamar's babies were "settlers," they brought the crime upon themselves (14 residents of Itamar have been killed by terrorists). It is hard to escape the feeling that had similar attacks occurred in, say, London or Paris, rather than a religious Zionist right-wing settlement in Samaria, the global reaction would undoubtedly have been totally different. Sderot, Ashkelon, Ashdod, Beersheba... All major southern Israel cities are under a heavy rocket offensive from Hamas-controlled Gaza. There are Jewish dead, babies wounded, schools and synagogues destroyed, cities and towns terrorized. But Israel as the most heavily bombed nation in the world never receives the Vatican's solidarity. Not only that, but the Church's officials compared Gaza, from where the terrorists fire on Israel, to a concentration camp.

There is only one historical precedent of a modern democracy besieged under rocket attacks. During the afternoon of Sept. 7, 1940, 348 Nazi bombers appeared over London. For the next 57 days, the city was bombed day and night. Fires consumed portions of the city. Residents sought shelter wherever they could find it — many fleeing to the underground that sheltered as many as 177,000 people during the night. Londoners, who had endured the blitz stoically, with British aplomb and courage, then had more than 1,200 V-1 bombs rain down on them from the skies, followed later by hundreds of larger V-2 missiles that gave no warning. The people of Israel are equally valiant, going about their daily lives knowing that killers might explode a bomb or rocket in any public place at any time.

The Vatican's blindness on terrorism against Israel was evident not only on Itamar and the rockets, but also in the case of suicide attacks during the Second Intifada or Oslo's war. As we documented in the book, the Pope in 2005 "forgot" to mention terrorism against Israel, while the Jewish State has been struck in the most familiar places by the suicide bombers: scores of young people and children, women and elderly incinerated on civilian buses; cafes and pizzerias destroyed; shopping malls turned into slaughterhouses; mothers and daughters killed in front of ice cream shops; families exterminated in their own beds; infants executed with a blow to the base of the skull; fruit markets blown to pieces; nightclubs eviscerated along with hundreds of students; seminarians murdered during their studies; husbands and wives killed in front of their children; brothers and sisters, grandparents and grandchildren murdered together; children murdered in their mothers' arms.

The terrorists have always selected their targets in Israel very carefully, to cause as much destruction as possible. One suicide bomber in Rishon Lezion massacred a group of elderly who were enjoying the cool air on a patio, where they had no protection. There are the shopping malls like in Efrat, pedestrian areas like in Hadera, bus stops like in Afula and Jerusalem, train stations like in Nahariya, pizzerias like in Karnei Shomron, nightclubs like the one in Tel Aviv, buses of students like in Gilo, bars and restaurants like in Herzliya, and cafes like in Haifa.

In Israel pieces of metal were added to the explosives in the terrorist's vest or backpack, with blasts often severing limbs completely. Many Israeli children have had their faces burned or their hands rendered useless; some have had their sight ruined forever. There are trembling elderly people, totally dependent. There are people who go insane and don't want to live anymore because they are haunted by the sound of the explosion, secluding themselves in their homes. Naturally, the focus has been mainly on the people killed in terror attacks, but more than eight times as many have been wounded. This is the true face of the war against the Jewish people: Jews scathed and scarred, living reminders of the Israeli 9/11. They require years of costly and complicated physical and mental rehabilitation. Israeli doctors estimate that 40% of the injured will have permanent disabilities. There are survivors of attacks who struggle even to get rid of the stench of death.

Some Israelis are still hospitalized with injuries sustained in suicide attacks years ago; many more require repeated hospital visits and multiple operations. Many are unable to work. Thousands of families have been forced to alter their lives to care for a wounded member. For all those killed, there are many, many more left alive but burned, scarred, blinded, hearing-impaired, or missing limbs. Many sustain fractures, vascular injuries, paralysis, or brain damage. There is no other conclusion to draw: when the deaths of so many Jewish innocents go so unacknowledged, it is because Jewish lives do not count. The most important lesson of Itamar is that the "civilized world" had already accepted and digested the perspective of a new Shoah. That night didn't generate any scandal in the Catholic conscience.

From Norwich to Itamar, the Jewish martyrs are an everlasting and heroic stain in the most horrible, theological blood libel. The doctrine which sees the Jews "superseded" by the Church. The Vatican said nothing about the dark night of Itamar. If the Church cannot talk, cannot bring herself to speak forcefully about Muslim anti-Semitism and anti-Jewish incitement, can it truly claim to have overcome the problem of anti-Semitism in its own communities? In its own heart? During the years preceding, and during the entire period of the Holocaust, the majority of Christians in Europe remained silent and became bystanders as the worst atrocities in history took place. Today, exactly as during Pius XII's time, there are only two possible reactions: being concerned and resisting, or being complacent and collaborating.

The Christmas message from Pope Pius XII in 1942 was incredibly generic; meanwhile the German Eintzagruppen were killing hundreds of thousands of Jews in the eastern territories, the Polish Jews were already entering en masse into the gas chambers of Belzec, Sobibor, Treblinka and Chelmmo, and in

Yugoslavia the Shoah was already a *fait accompli*. There have been single Churches which denounced the Holocaust, like the French bishops, the Orthodox Church in Bulgaria, the Greek Orthodox and the Protestants in Norway. But the Vatican's behavior during the Second World War was that of indifference and silence, despite some cases of bravery and solidarity with the Jewish people.

The German Catholics abandoned the Jews by helping the SS to trace Jewish genealogy through their archives. In 1936 the paper Klerusblatt, the official bulletin of the Bavarian Catholic bishops, praised the Nuremberg laws because it is a "preservation of the German blood."[235] When the Church spoke loudly and clearly, Hitler had to stop the euthanasia program T4. Hundreds of Catholic priests followed the German troops in the killing fields of Soviet Union. In Slovak a Catholic priest, Josef Tiso, helped Adolf Eichmann deport the local Jews. In 1942 the local bishops approved the Shoah of the Jews who had not been able to "recognize the Redentor." In Croatia the priests took part in the genocide, and 40,000 Jews were killed under the reign of "Fra Satan," the priest Miroslav Filipovic-Majstorovic. In 1897 the magazine Civiltà Cattolica, whose pages have the Vatican's official approval, declared that "a Jew remains a Jew in every place," and in 1936, after the Nuremberg laws, it proclaimed that the Jews were "parasites," and that "Judaism is a foreign body that produces irritation and reactions in the guest organism." Cardinal Adolf Beltram, head of the German church, at the peak of the Shoah attacked the "pernicious Jewish influence on the German culture." The Bishop of Sarajevo, Ivan Saric, in 1941 attacked "Jewish greed." In Slovenia the Bishop of the capital Lubiana, Gregory Rozman, spoke against the "Jewish conspiracy." The churches provided the conceptual framework for the perception of the Jew as less than human, or as inhuman, devilish and satanic, as well as being traitors, murderers, plague, pollution, filth, and insects.

---

[235] "A Moral Reckoning" by Daniel Goldhagen

Few bishops openly and bravely opposed the killings: the French Delay, the Austrian Gfollner, the Polish Hland and the Croatian Stepinac. Only in two cases did the Church help the Jews at a regional level: Berlin and Italy, where some Jews found refuge in the Vatican. Daniel Goldhagen writes that the Catholic church on the Holocaust has guilt deeper than that of Julius Streicher, the German journalist in charge of Nazi propaganda. In December of 1942 the major leaders of the Evangelical Church published a letter that denied to the Jews the salvation through baptism, calling them "enemies of the Reich."

After the Holocaust, the Vatican helped found a shelter for the major war criminals: Adolf Eichmann, architect of the Shoah; Franz Stangl, commander of Sobibor and Treblinka; Kurt Christman, commander of the Sonderkommand 10a; Walter Rauff, inventor of the mobile gas chambers; Klaus Barbie, the Butcher of Lione; Ante Pavelic, head of the Croatian fascists, and Joseph Mengele, the doctor of Auschwitz, who fled through Italy with the assistance of the Catholic network. Evil dominated the Christian indifference toward the Jews. But the Vatican could also have redeemed its relations with Israel through rediscovering the "righteous among the nations" tradition. These are the Christians who risked their lives to help Jews during the Holocaust. Their actions shed a light on the dark star of the Holocaust.

When the Yad Vashem memorial in Jerusalem was established to commemorate the six million Jews murdered, the Knesset added another task to the Holocaust Remembrance Authority's mission: to honor those non-Jews who had taken great risks to save Jews during the persecution. The motivation for the establishment of this unique program was a deep sense of gratitude toward the tiny minority that stood by the Jewish people, but there seems to have been an added dimension. In a world where Auschwitz had become a real possibility, the Jewish people and the survivors needed to hang on to some hope for mankind, something that would enable them to maintain their faith in human values and rebuild their lives after having witnessed an unprecedented moral collapse.

During the Holocaust the Christian mainstream watched as their former Jewish neighbors were rounded up and killed; some collaborated with the perpetrators and most benefited from the expropriation of the Jews' property. But a Christian, brave group of people felt that the persecuted Jews were part of their universe of obligation, and that it was their duty to act.

Several on the guest list are from Holland, where 25,000 Jews were hidden by their compatriots or helped by a strong underground network and the Dutch Reform Church. In the small city of Liczkowce, father Michael Kujata, sheltered a Jewish girl, Anita Helfgott. When the ghetto of Brzezany was destroyed, Mark and Klara Zipper were saved by Julian Baran and his Catholic family. The future head of the US anti-defamation league, Abraham Foxman, was saved by a Catholic lady. Jan and Zofia Bartoszewicz saved the famous poet Avraham Sutzkever. Maryla Abramowicz-Walska, later known as "the white angel of Vilnius," saved many Jews, including the historian Mark Dworzecki and the poet Shmerl Kaczerginski.

There were non Jews killed for protesting against the pogroms. In Mlawa all the citizens were asked to see a public execution of 50 Jews. One of the locals interrupted the killings crying, "You are spilling innocent blood." He was put to death with the Jews. Who knows his name? In Warsaw, few Churchmen helped the Jews. Marceli Godlewski was priest in the Church of Ognissanti, and saved the famous doctor Ludwig Hirszfeld. In Berlin the Protestant reverend Heinrich Gruber saved many Jews by giving them "Aryan" documents. In France, Catholic institutions provided help and shelter to hundreds of Jews. Archbishop of Nice, Paul Remond, was one of the most generous during the Holocaust. In Belgium there was the Protestant Marc Boegner. Reverend Henri Reynders saved 320 Jewish children. In Assisi, two Italian priests, Bishop

Nicolini and Father Niccaci, saved 300 Jews. In Budapest Father Jakab Railc saved 150 Jews.

Israel is still in the process of establishing the terms of its existence, and significant currents in the Arab world still regard Israel's existence as temporary. Israel's current struggle for its own future gives them a chance to redeem their past mistakes. The Jewish people now face the prospect of a new Holocaust at the hands of Iran, which President Mahmoud Ahmadinejad threatens as brazenly as ever did Hitler. Emanuel Ringelblum, the great historian of Polish Jewry who was killed during the Holocaust, noted that during the war the "Polish clergy was distinguished for its remarkably anti-Semitic attitude. When... the blood of Jewish students was shed... when anti-Semitic savages rioted... the clergy either kept silent or approved these deeds..." Those words, pronounced by a hero of the Warsaw ghetto, could be used also today for the Vatican's indifference to Israel's mortal siege. And just as in World War II, Catholic communities are hostage to an evil power that proposes to wipe out the Jewish people, and the first concern of the Church is to maintain its ministry under adverse conditions. Just as in World War II, some elements of the Church make common cause with this evil power to buy temporary security for their own communities.

In 1942, the Nazis gathered in a villa outside Berlin to adopt "the Final Solution of the Jewish People." Then anti-Semites wanted to make the world Judenrein, free of Jews. In 2012, anti-Semites want to make the world "Judenstaatrein," free of a Jewish State. The immense, indescribable horror of the Holocaust which caused the annihilation of one third of the world's Jewish population must continue to profoundly shake the Christian world; it must challenge the Western conscience; it must lead to theological doubts; it must restore to Judaism, in the Christian consciousness, the dignity of a millennial faith of a covenantal people in its biblical land — a concept which for centuries was fought against and denied by the Catholic Church. Jews were called Antichrists, avaricious, blasphemers, cheats, circumcisers, cowards, crucifiers, deicides, desecrators of the Host, devils.

That is why Pius XII's behavior during the Holocaust has a very deep resonance in our day. Did the Church learn that the road to Hell is paved with silence? And next time, will Christians be brave, or cowardly, in face of evil, should it be rockets on Sderot, suicide bombers in Hadera, slitting throats in Itamar, missiles on Tel Aviv or the old anti-Semitism raising its head again in Europe? If not, the charge of Auschwitz's anti-Semitism will still ring true. A sour rain is falling, once again, on our heads now that the Holocaust is going to be consigned to "the last century" due to the natural deaths of the last survivors, and that will be the first step from history to story, from story to dream and from dream to amnesia. And as history has taught us, while it begins with Jews, it doesn't end with them. After centuries of anti-Semitism spawned by the Church, modern-day Christians have the religious, moral and political obligation to help make the world a safer place for Jews.

Will Israel be forsaken, again?

CPSIA information can be obtained at www.ICGtesting.com
Printed in the USA
LVOW01s1710100714

393764LV00020B/1282/P